CAPTIVATING AUDIENCES WITH WORDS

Captivating Audiences With Words

Rayan Musk

Noble Publishing

Contents

1

INDEX

3.1 The principles of persuasion and their application in communication

3.2 Building credibility and trust with your audience

3.3 Utilizing rhetorical devices to enhance persuasive communication

3.4 Persuasive speeches and writings

Chapter 4: The Impact of Language and Tone

4.1 Exploring the nuances of language and its emotional impact

4.2 Choosing the right tone for different audiences and contexts

4.3 The role of language in creating a memorable and lasting impression

4.4 Practical exercises to enhance linguistic versatility

Chapter 5: Public Speaking Techniques

5.1 Overcoming fear and anxiety associated with public speaking

5.2 Body language and non-verbal communication tips

5.3 Capturing attention from the start and maintaining engagement

5.4 Q&A strategies and handling unexpected challenges

Chapter 6: Leveraging Technology and Multimedia

6.1 Incorporating visuals and multimedia for enhanced impact

6.2 Utilizing technology to reach wider audiences

6.3 The dos and don'ts of integrating technology into speeches and presentations

6.4 Successful use of multimedia in communication

Chapter 7: Evolving as a Master Communicator

7.1 Continual improvement and learning in the art of communication

7.2 Seeking and incorporating feedback for personal growth

7.3 Staying adaptable to evolving communication trends

7.4 Inspiring others through your words: the responsibility of a captivating communicator

2

Introduction

In the immense domain of human correspondence, the force of words has shown to be an unrivaled power, equipped for significantly shaping considerations, lighting feelings, and rising above the limits of reality. As we explore the steadily developing scene of language, one consistent remaining parts: the craft of enamoring crowds with words. In this investigation, we set out on an excursion through the complex embroidery of language, diving into the subtleties that change simple sentences into enamoring stories, talks, and articulations that reverberate across ages.

At the center of this excursion lies the significant comprehension that words are not simple vessels of data but rather vessels of importance, conveying the heaviness of human experience, culture, and intelligence. From the old looks of progress to the computerized chronicles of the present, the composed and expressed word has been a channel for the transmission of information, the conservation of stories, and the enunciation of thoughts that rise above the constraints of the prompt second.

Dazzling crowds with words is a work of art that reaches out past the simple game plan of letters; a catalytic cycle changes dynamic considerations into substantial feelings, associates unique personalities, and shapes the shared mindset. As we unwind the strings of this craftsmanship, we end up in the domain of way of talking, the antiquated discipline that investigates the specialty of influence and expert articulation. From Aristotle's compositions on influence to the speech ability of incredible pioneers since forever ago, way of talking highlights the immortal mission to dominate the specialty of words that move hearts and brains.

The excursion into dazzling crowds with words is a multi-layered investigation that incorporates the mechanics of language as well as the significant brain science of human association. From the selection of words to the rhythm of conveyance, communicators become modelers of encounters, building spans among speaker and audience, author and peruser. The harmonious dance of words and feelings makes a space where thoughts take off, starting motivation and prompting change.

In the computerized age, where consideration is a sought after cash, the test of enrapturing crowds has arrived at new levels. The whirlwind of data barraging people day to day requires a recalibration of customary ways to deal with correspondence. From the succinct polish of microcontent to the vivid profundity of long-structure narrating, the contemporary communicator should explore a scene where curtness and profundity coincide. As we analyze the procedures utilized by ace communicators in the computerized domain, we uncover the combination of innovation and manner of speaking, leading to another time of etymological development.

The force of narrating arises as a focal subject in the craft of enamoring crowds with words. Past the spread of realities, stories weave an embroidery of human experience, injecting accounts with appeal, sympathy, and reverberation. From the fireside stories of old clans to the realistic stories of the present, narrating stays a powerful vehicle for the transmission of values, the investigation of character, and the development of shared importance.

Language, as a living element, develops close by the consistently moving sands of culture and society. The dictionary extends, expressions flourish, and phonetic patterns arise as impressions of the shared perspective. To dazzle crowds with words requires a sharp consciousness of these etymological flows, a capacity to ride the influxes of social importance while likewise rocking the boat. In investigating the harmonious connection among language and culture, we uncover the unique transaction that shapes the recurring pattern of public talk.

The appeal of manner of speaking reaches out past customary stages to the domain of advanced media, where forces to be reckoned with, thought pioneers, and content makers employ the ability to shape assessments and prepare networks. The democratization of data has changed crowds into dynamic members, obscuring the lines among speaker and audience. In this participatory scene, the craft of spellbinding crowds requires a comprehension of the intuitive idea of correspondence, where criticism circles, remarks, and offers become essential parts of the discussion.

As we explore the immense expanse of language, we experience the meaning of validness in enthralling crowds with words. In a period where suspicion towards conventional organizations is on the ascent, the genuine voice turns into a guide of trust. Realness rises above the cleaned facade of correspondence, welcoming crowds into the crude and certified human experience. From the weakness of individual narrating to the unfiltered legitimacy of unscripted minutes, communicators who embrace realness produce a more profound association with their crowd.

The convergence of language and feeling turns into a point of convergence in our investigation, as we dive into the manners by which words summon sentiments and mix the profundities of the human spirit. Whether through the musical rhythm of verse, the emotive force of similitudes, or the suggestive reverberation of painstakingly picked phrases, the profound scene turns into the material whereupon communicators paint their stories. The dominance of profound reverberation arises as a foundation in the specialty of enrapturing crowds, where the capacity to evoke giggling, tears, or thought turns into a demonstration of the communicator's ability.

In the period of data over-burden, the specialty of straightforwardness turns into a core value in dazzling crowds with words. The capacity to distil complex thoughts into available language, to convey significance with lucidity, denotes the distinction between simple correspondence and effective talk. From the tastefulness of a very much created title to the lucidity of a compact message, straightforwardness turns into an essential device in catching and holding crowd consideration.

The globalized idea of present day correspondence welcomes us to investigate the comprehensiveness of enamoring crowds with words. Across societies and dialects, certain accounts, prime examples, and logical gadgets rise above borders, resounding with the common human experience. As we look at the diverse allure of narrating, humor, and widespread subjects, we uncover the strings that mesh mankind into an embroidery of interconnected stories.

The advanced period has birthed new mediums and organizations, extending the material whereupon communicators paint their words. From the reduced down brightness of web-based entertainment to the vivid scenes of augmented reality, the development of innovation presents novel open doors and difficulties in charming crowds. The combination of words with visuals, sound, and intuitive components opens new boondocks in narrating, requesting a reconsideration of conventional correspondence standards.

Chasing after enrapturing crowds with words, moral contemplations arise as core values that shape the effect of correspondence. The obligation that accompanies the ability to impact requests an upright methodology, where communicators explore the scarcely discernible difference among influence and control, validness and guile. In a time of deception and disinformation, the moral communicator turns into a steward of truth, using words with honesty and reason.

The embroidery of spellbinding crowds with words is a dynamic, consistently developing mosaic that mirrors the kaleidoscope of human articulation. From the old speakers who moved jams in the marketplace to the contemporary powerhouses who order computerized stages, the pith of enrapturing crowds stays an immortal pursuit. As we cross the scenes of way of talking, narrating, validness, feeling, straightforwardness, and morals, we reveal the mind boggling dance of language that ties people in shared snapshots of significance.

In this investigation, we welcome you to set out on an excursion through the maze of words, where the speculative chemistry of correspondence unfurls in horde structures. Together, we unwind the privileged insights of enrapturing crowds, finding the ageless standards and imaginative systems that rise above the limits of time and culture. Go along with us in this odyssey of words, where the ability to enrapture changes language into a no nonsense power that resounds across the ages.

Chapter 1

The Power of Words

Language, the unpredictable embroidered artwork of human correspondence, winds around its impact through the structure holding the system together, shaping considerations, feelings, and activities. Words, the structure blocks of language, have a significant power that rises above their simple phonetic presence. They have the ability to rouse, to instigate, to mend, and to hurt. In the tremendous domain of human experience, the force of words arises as a power both unpretentious and imposing, equipped for embellishment fates and reshaping the shapes of the real world.

At its center, language is an instrument for conveying meaning, a scaffold that interfaces minds across the gorge of individual cognizance. The force of words lies in their capacity to verbalize contemplations, sentiments, and thoughts, changing conceptual ideas into substantial articulations. Whether spoken or composed, words act as vessels for the transmission of information, culture, and insight through ages. They epitomize the quintessence of human experience, conveying the heaviness of history and the commitment representing things to come.

However, the genuine strength of words stretches out past their educational capability. Words have a groundbreaking energy, fit for molding insights and impacting perspectives. A solitary expression can ignite the blazes of unrest, prompting developments that rock the boat and usher in a period of progress. On the other hand, words can be employed as weapons, causing wounds that putrefy in the openings of the brain, leaving scars that get through lengthy after the reverberations of discourse have blurred.

Consider the expressiveness of incredible speakers who have influenced the course of history with their words. From the red hot way of talking of Winston Churchill during The Second Great War to the ardent addresses of Martin Luther Lord Jr. during the Social liberties Development, words have been the impetuses for stupendous changes in human undertakings. These pioneers outfit the force of language to prepare masses, to light the flash of trust, and to electrify aggregate activity.

In writing, the composed word expects an extraordinary job, rising above the limits of existence. Creators, through the speculative chemistry of language, make universes that exist past the bounds of the real world. The books of Dickens transport perusers to the abrasive roads of Victorian London, while the verse of Rumi welcomes thought in the domains of the otherworldly and the superb. Through words, writing turns into a mirror mirroring the human condition, an immortal demonstration of the all inclusiveness of the human experience.

However, to whom much is given, much will be expected. The effect of words isn't generally harmless, and the potential for abuse poses a potential threat. History demonstrates the veracity of cases where promulgation and detest discourse have been utilized to plant the seeds of disunity, to dehumanize whole populaces, and to legitimize monstrosities. The force of words, when bridled for noxious purposes, can be an intense weapon of control and control.

In the advanced age, the expansion of data through different channels enhances the impact of words. Web-based entertainment stages, media sources, and online gatherings act as landmarks where contending stories strive for incomparability. In this bedlam of voices, the force of words is amplified, forming general assessment, affecting political talk, and trim social standards. The viral spread of hashtags and trademarks turns into a demonstration of the capacity of words to stir developments and to ignite worldwide discussions.

Also, the advanced time acquaints new aspects with the force of words with the approach of man-made consciousness and normal language handling. Robotized frameworks can now create human-like text, obscuring the lines among legitimacy and stratagem. As calculations curate content and shape online collaborations, the impact of words reaches out past human organization, bringing up issues about the moral ramifications of phonetic advances.

In relational connections, the force of words is apparent in the elements of correspondence. A painstakingly picked state can possibly repair broken bonds, to communicate love and understanding, and to manufacture associations that endure everyday hardship. On the other hand, the heaviness of a thoughtless word can break connections, abandoning a path of disdain and misjudging. In the domain of feelings, words become the brushstrokes that paint the material of human associations.

The force of words is additionally manifest in the domain of self-talk and interior exchange. The accounts we build inside our brains, the narratives we tell ourselves, shape our self-discernment and impact our activities. Positive certifications can be a wellspring of strengthening, cultivating versatility and fearlessness. On the other hand, a blast of pessimistic self-talk can turn into an inevitable outcome, sabotaging potential and frustrating self-awareness.

Language, as a dynamic and developing element, mirrors the qualities and standards of a general public. The force of words is personally attached to issues of portrayal and inclusivity. The language we use shapes our impression of the world and educates our comprehension regarding different personalities. Comprehensive language perceives the significance of portrayal, recognizing the nobility and humankind, everything being equal. On the other hand, exclusionary language propagates generalizations, minimizing specific gatherings and sustaining fundamental disparities.

In the lawful area, the accuracy of language is fundamental. Regulations and resolutions are fastidiously created to pass the aim of administrators and on to lay out the boundaries of equity. The understanding of legitimate texts relies on the subtleties of language, and the force of words in this setting can decide the course of equity. Legitimate talk turns into a landmark where lawyers use words as weapons, looking to convince judges and juries through the craft of argumentation.

Strict texts, worshipped as consecrated, are archives of heavenly insight and moral direction. The force of words in strict settings stretches out past the exacting to the powerful, forming convictions, customs, and moral structures. Hallowed sacred writings act as a wellspring of motivation and an aide for moral direct, their words reverberating through the hallways of confidence and impacting the existences of devotees.

In the domain of training, the force of words is apparent during the time spent educating and learning. Instructors, through the talented utilization of language, can light interest, to move inventiveness, and to give information that rises above the limits of the homeroom. On the other hand, the effect of negative words or deterring language can smother scholarly development and dissolve the certainty of students.

The force of words isn't restricted to the domains of high way of talking or formal talk; it pervades the regular collaborations that comprise the embroidery of human life. In the closeness of individual connections, words become the cash of adoration, compassion, and association. The trading of commitments in marriage, the consolation of a companion in the midst of hardship, the chuckling divided between mates — these minutes are totally woven together by the force of words.

However, the fleeting idea of verbally expressed words represents a test. Once expressed, words can't be implied, and their effect waits in the hearts and brains of the people who get them. The obligation of communicators, thusly, is to employ their words with care and goal, perceiving the getting through outcomes of language.

In the computerized age, the lastingness of composed words takes on another aspect. Texts, messages, and virtual entertainment posts can be safeguarded endlessly, their life span intensifying the possible effect of words. The computerized effects we have behind turned into a demonstration of the force of words to shape our virtual characters and to impact the view of others.

The force of words is likewise intrinsic in the specialty of influence. Manner of speaking, the craft of viable correspondence, use the powerful capability of words to impact assessments and influence crowds. From political talks to promoting efforts, the essential utilization of language plans to get explicit reactions and to shape the story for the communicator. The influential ability lies in the capacity to approach issues, to bring out feelings, and to develop unquestionable claims that reverberate with the main interest group.

In the field of public talk, the force of words is exemplified in the conflict of contending stories. Issues of civil rights, ecological maintainability, and basic liberties are challenged with the help of language. Advocates utilize words as weapons in the fight for hearts and brains, looking to prepare public help and to impact change on a foundational level. The force of words turns into an impetus for social developments, driving advancement and testing the designs of imbalance.

The force of words isn't restricted to the outside domain of cultural talk; it broadens internal, molding the scene of individual awareness. The accounts we develop about ourselves, the tales we accept, impact our self-discernment and guide our activities. The force of self-confirmation, the cognizant decision to express uplifting statements and energy to oneself, can be a groundbreaking power in conquering difficulties and cultivating flexibility.

On the other hand, the assimilation of negative stories, the persevering redundancy of self-uncertainty and analysis, can turn into a deliberate jail. The force of words to shape our self-idea highlights the significance of developing a careful and sympathetic inward exchange. By perceiving the effect of our self-talk, we gain the organization to reevaluate our stories and to sustain a really enabling relationship with ourselves.

In the domain of imagination, the force of words is tackled by craftsmen, artists, and narrators. Language turns into the range with which authors paint distinctive scenes of creative mind. The reminiscent force of verse rises above the strict, welcoming perusers to investigate the profundities of feeling and the subtleties of the human experience. Through the speculative chemistry of words, specialists make universes that reverberate with perusers, manufacturing associations that rise above the limits of existence.

The force of words is obvious in the domain of web-based entertainment, where the quickness of correspondence enhances the effect of language. Tweets, announcements, and hashtags can possibly shape popular assessment, touch off developments, and impact political talk. The quickness of web-based entertainment messages requires compactness and accuracy, accentuating the force of painstakingly picked words to convey meaning and get reactions.

Be that as it may, the fast speed of online correspondence likewise presents difficulties. The viral spread of falsehood, the enhancement of disruptive manner of speaking, and the disintegration of subtlety for drama are appearances of the situation with two sides that is the force of words in the computerized age. As society wrestles with the ramifications of online correspondence, the obligation to employ words morally and capably becomes vital.

In the journey for genuineness, the force of words expects a focal job. Genuine correspondence rises above the stratagem of performative language, embracing weakness and straightforwardness. The validness of words resounds with crowds, cultivating certified associations and causing trust. In a period where suspicion and negativity flourish, the force of valid correspondence turns into a guide of genuineness in an ocean of clamor.

The force of words reaches out to the domain of memory and recognition. Through composed and spoken accounts, people and social orders safeguard the aggregate memory of shared encounters. The accounts we tell about the past shape how we might interpret history and illuminate our sense regarding personality. The force of words to memorialize occasions, to recognize lives, and to send social legacy highlights their job as caretakers of aggregate memory.

However, the flexibility of memory presents intricacies. The specific utilization of words can shape authentic accounts to serve specific plans, mutilating reality and propagating deceptions. The ability to shape aggregate memory through the control of language highlights the moral basic to move toward history with a guarantee to truth and exactness.

In the domain of science, the force of words is instrumental in the correspondence of perplexing thoughts and revelations. Analysts, through the fastidious enunciation of their discoveries, add to the headway of information and the development of human getting it.

The accuracy of logical language, its ability to convey subtlety and explicitness, upgrades the thoroughness of request and works with joint effort among researchers.

Nonetheless, the force of logical language additionally presents provokes in its openness to the more extensive public. The obscure idea of specialized language can make hindrances to understanding, distancing the people who need particular information. Overcoming any barrier between logical talk and public perception requires a cognizant work to convey complex thoughts in a way that is clear, captivating, and comprehensive.

The force of words is inherently attached to social articulation and phonetic variety. Across the globe, different etymological customs give testimony regarding the rich woven artwork of human articulation. Every language epitomizes extraordinary points of view, typifying the social subtleties and verifiable accounts of its speakers. The conservation of semantic variety turns into an essential part of protecting the aggregate legacy of humankind.

Notwithstanding globalization, the power elements innate in language become evident. Prevailing dialects use impact on the worldwide stage, forming global talk and saturating social products. The influence of phonetic authority brings up issues about value and portrayal, highlighting the need to celebrate and safeguard etymological variety as a fundamental feature of social extravagance.

In the domain of discretion, the force of words becomes the dominant focal point as countries explore the intricacies of global relations. Ambassadors, through the specialty of exchange and discourse, look to fabricate extensions and resolve clashes. The accuracy of discretionary language, its ability to pass subtlety and on to explore strategic subtleties, is fundamental in cultivating common comprehension and collaboration among countries.

Alternately, the abuse of language in political settings can have sweeping outcomes. The heightening of way of talking, the utilization of incendiary language, and the breakdown of correspondence channels add to political emergencies and international pressures. The force of words in strategy highlights the fragile harmony among decisiveness and tact, the requirement for key correspondence in exploring the complexities of foreign relations.

1.1 Introduction to the impact of words on audiences

The effect of words on crowds is a subject of significant importance in the domain of correspondence. Words, as the key units of language, have an innate ability to shape discernments, summon feelings, and impact the contemplations and activities of people. This power isn't bound to formal addresses or scholarly works; it pervades the texture of regular cooperations, from individual discussions to the huge scene of computerized correspondence.

The investigation of how words reverberate with crowds digs into the complexities of human brain science, social elements, and the advancing idea of correspondence in the cutting edge period.

At its embodiment, the effect of words on crowds is established in the capacity of language to convey meaning and make mutual perspective. Correspondence is a unique cycle wherein words act as vehicles for thoughts, feelings, and data. Whether spoken or composed, words capability as scaffolds that interface the source of a message with its collector. The selection of words, their tone, and the setting where they are conveyed all add to the manner in which crowds decipher and answer correspondence.

With regards to public talking, the effect of words is amplified, as speakers tackle the force of language to address and draw in different crowds. A very much created discourse can possibly rouse, propel, and prepare people toward a typical reason. From memorable discourses that have energized social developments to contemporary TED Talks that spellbind worldwide crowds, the specialty of public talking highlights the extraordinary impact of words on shared perspective.

The effect of words not set in stone by their educational substance yet in addition by their profound reverberation. Genuinely charged words have the ability to evoke solid responses, making an enduring impact on crowds. Whether through the blending language of a political pioneer mobilizing a country or the powerful expressions of a narrator bringing out sympathy, feelings shape the manner in which crowds interface with and incorporate the messages they get.

Social subtleties further shape the effect of words, as language is pervaded with social implications and implications. Similar arrangement of words might convey different weight and importance in assorted social settings. Understanding the social responsive qualities of a group of people is significant in compelling correspondence, as words that resound decidedly in one culture may unexpectedly distance or outrage in another. The effect of words, subsequently, requires a nuanced familiarity with social variety to cultivate comprehensive and deferential correspondence.

In the domain of writing, the effect of words stretches out past the prompt snapshot of perusing to leave an enduring engraving on the personalities of perusers. Writers, through their authority of language, make universes that perusers occupy, characters they understand, and accounts that reverberate with their own encounters. The force of narrating lies in its capacity to rise above individual viewpoints, cultivating a common association among different crowds through the comprehensiveness of human stories.

The approach of computerized correspondence has introduced another time where the effect of words is intensified and sped up. Virtual entertainment stages, websites, and online gatherings furnish people with extraordinary chances to impart their contemplations and insights with a worldwide crowd. The viral idea of content on the web highlights the potential for words to quickly spread, impacting public talk and molding aggregate discernments.

Be that as it may, the computerized scene additionally presents difficulties to the effect of words, as the curtness and quickness of online correspondence can prompt the distortion of complicated issues. The viral spread of deception, the closed quarters framed by algorithmic substance curation, and the disintegration of subtlety for drama all add to the advancing elements of the effect of words in the computerized age. Exploring this scene requires an elevated familiarity with the likely results of words in an interconnected and quickly impacting world.

In relational connections, the effect of words is profoundly entwined with the elements of human association. Successful correspondence inside connections relies on the capacity to offer viewpoints and feelings plainly, to listen compassionately, and to pick words that cultivate understanding and trust. Alternately, the indiscreet or harmful utilization of words can strain connections, making fractures that might be trying to repair. The effect of words in private cooperations highlights the significance of relational abilities in supporting solid and significant associations.

The force of words is likewise clear in the domain of influence, where people and substances try to impact the convictions and ways of behaving of others. Enticing correspondence includes the essential utilization of words to construct a convincing case, address counterarguments, and appeal to the qualities and feelings of the interest group. Whether in promoting, political missions, or support endeavors, the effect of words on influence is a unique exchange between way of talking, brain science, and the developing scene of popular assessment.

Moral contemplations assume an essential part in understanding the effect of words, especially in settings where falsehood, control, and destructive language flourish. The obligation to impart morally includes a guarantee to honesty, straight-forwardness, and the evasion of language that might induce hurt or propagate segregation. As innovation keeps on propelling, the moral components of the effect of words gain unmistakable quality, requiring carefulness in protecting the respectability of correspondence in the computerized circle.

In the instructive space, the effect of words reaches out to the most common way of educating and learning. Instructors, through the capable utilization of language, can connect with understudies, convey complex ideas, and motivate an adoration for learning. The effect of words in schooling isn't restricted to the transmission of data however envelops the development of decisive reasoning, imagination, and a long lasting interest for information.

The language utilized in instructive settings shapes the scholarly and profound encounters of understudies, impacting their perspectives toward learning and the world.

With regards to character and self-discernment, the effect of words is significant. The accounts we build about ourselves, both inside and because of outside impacts, shape our self-idea and guide our activities. Positive attestations and self-enabling language can support confidence and flexibility, while pessimistic self-talk can add to self-uncertainty and breaking point self-awareness. Understanding the effect of words on self-insight highlights the significance of encouraging a positive and certifying inner exchange.

The effect of words in the legitimate domain is apparent in the accuracy expected in the making of regulations, contracts, and lawful contentions. Legitimate language is described by its explicitness, subtlety, and meticulousness, as the understanding of lawful texts can have sweeping outcomes. The effect of words in legitimate settings stretches out to court manner of speaking, where attorneys utilize language de-cisively to construct cases, convince judges and juries, and explore the complexities of the equity framework.

Strict and otherworldly practices likewise feature the effect of words, as hallowed texts and lessons act as guides for moral lead and profound development. The words inside strict settings hold groundbreaking power, molding the convictions, ceremonies, and moral structures of networks. The effect of strict language isn't restricted to individual confidence yet reaches out to its impact on social standards, cultural qualities, and the more extensive texture of human development.

The effect of words on crowds is a diverse peculiarity that rises above disciplin-ary limits. From the domains of writing and craftsmanship to the fields of public talking, advanced correspondence, and relational connections, words shape the manner in which people see, comprehend, and draw in with the world. Perceiving the effect of words requires a comprehensive methodology that thinks about the transaction of language, culture, feeling, and morals in the different settings where correspondence unfurls.

As we explore the intricacies of correspondence in an interconnected worldwide society, a consciousness of the effect of words turns into a foundation of mindful and successful talk. The advancing idea of language, innovation, and human collaboration highlights the powerful exchange of variables that add to the effect of words on crowds. In embracing this intricacy, people, communicators, and social orders can outfit the force of words to encourage figuring out, compassion, and positive change in the different embroidered artwork of human experience.

1.2 Historical examples of speeches and writings that captivated masses

Since forever ago, certain discourses and compositions have risen above their worldly settings, resounding across ages and enthralling the majority with their significant effect. These stylistic and artistic works of art have the ability to rouse, activate, and shape the course of history. Looking at verifiable instances of such discourses and works offers experiences into the specialty of influence, the elements of authority, and the persevering through impact of expressiveness.

One of the most famous instances of a discourse that enthralled the majority is Martin Luther Lord Jr's. "I Have a Fantasy" discourse, conveyed during the Walk on Washington for Occupations and Opportunity on August 28, 1963. Lord's smooth enunciation of his fantasy for a racially coordinated and agreeable America hit home for millions. His strong utilization of illustration, redundancy, and musical rhythm conveyed a dream of racial balance that rose above the quick social equality battle, settling on it an immortal decision for equity and fortitude.

Also, Winston Churchill's talks during The Second Great War are praised for their capacity to elevate and stir the English nation despite misfortune. Churchill's renowned "We Will Battle on the Sea shores" discourse, followed through on June 4, 1940, is a mixing illustration of his rhetorical ability. Even with the impending danger of Nazi intrusion, Churchill's resistant manner of speaking and steady purpose ingrained a feeling of public solidarity and flexibility. His talks turned into an energizing sob for the English public and, likewise, for every one of the people who opposed the oppression of one party rule.

Abraham Lincoln's Gettysburg Address, followed through on November 19, 1863, is one more verifiable model that features the effect of succinct and strong language. In the result of a fierce Nationwide conflict fight, Lincoln conveyed a discourse that rose above a simple commitment function. With a simple 272 words, he communicated the significant meaning of saving a country "imagined in Freedom, and devoted to the suggestion that all men are made equivalent." The Gettysburg Address is loved for its curtness, clearness, and persevering through reverberation as a demonstration of the getting through standards of a majority rule government.

Moving past rhetoric, the force of the composed word is exemplified by Thomas Paine's "Sound judgment," distributed in 1776 during the American Upset. Paine's handout assumed an essential part in mobilizing support for American freedom from English rule. His reasonable and convincing language contended for the intrinsic right of the American provinces to self-administration, contacting an expansive crowd and catalyzing a groundswell of public opinion for freedom.

In the field of writing, Harriet Beecher Stowe's "Uncle Tom's Lodge" stands apart as a work that charmed the majority as well as touched off an intense abolitionist development in the US. Distributed in 1852, Stowe's original portrayed the brutal real factors of subjection and the ethical basic to annihilate this foundation. The close to home effect of her story arrived at perusers on an individual level, provoking a boundless reassessment of perspectives toward subjection and adding to the heightening pressures that prompted the American Nationwide conflict.

The force of addresses to excite whole countries is obvious in the manner of speaking of Sir Winston Churchill, during The Second Great War as well as in his popular "Iron Drape" discourse conveyed in Fulton, Missouri, on Walk 5, 1946. In this location, Churchill cautioned of the arising Cold Conflict and the philosophical split between the majority rule West and the socialist East. The clear symbolism of an "iron shade" sliding across Europe turned into a strong illustration that reverberated internationally, molding impression of the international scene for quite a long time.

Nelson Mandela's debut address as Leader of South Africa on May 10, 1994, is one more model of a discourse that encapsulated a country experiencing significant change. Following quite a while of politically-sanctioned racial segregation, Mandela's discourse underlined compromise, solidarity, and the quest for equity. His message of pardoning and inclusivity resounded with individuals of South Africa as well as with the worldwide local area, representing an encouraging sign for a more brilliant, more impartial future.

An alternate feature of spellbinding the majority should be visible in the composed expression of Anne Forthright. Her journal, composed while in stowing away during the Holocaust, gives an impactful and individual record of the human expense of oppression. Anne's genuine and contemplative composing has contacted perusers around the world, offering a distinct sign of the strength of the human soul notwithstanding misfortune. Her words keep on instructing, rouse, and incite reflection on the outcomes of contempt and bigotry.

The effect of discourses isn't restricted to political or wartime settings; they reach out to the domain of social liberties battles. Malcolm X's "Message to the Grass Roots," followed through on November 10, 1963, underlined the requirement for self-assurance and strengthening inside the African American people group. His energetic way of talking tested winning standards and pushed for an extreme re-examination of the social and political designs that propagated racial imbalance.

In an alternate social and verifiable setting, Mahatma Gandhi's discourses during India's battle for freedom exhibited the force of peaceful opposition. His location at the Salt Walk in 1930 and the Quit India discourse in 1942 highlighted the standards of truth, peacefulness, and common noncompliance.

Gandhi's expressiveness and obligation to equity reverberated with the Indian masses as well as with worldwide crowds, adding to an extraordinary change in the battle against expansionism.

The effect of words on masses isn't bound to discourses and compositions in the English language. Fidel Castro's addresses, conveyed in Spanish during the Cuban Upheaval, mobilized the Cuban nation against the severe system of Fulgencio Batista. Castro's energetic rhetoric and key utilization of language developed a progressive soul that at last prompted the defeat of Batista's administration.

The scholarly works of Gabriel Garcia Marquez, especially "100 Years of Isolation," significantly affect perusers around the world. Marquez's supernatural authenticity, well established in Latin American history and culture, has caught the creative mind of ages. His words weave an embroidery of mind boggling characters and occasions, offering a special point of view on the human condition that rises above social and phonetic limits.

With regards to orientation uniformity and ladies' privileges, the effect of words is clear in Simone de Beauvoir's fundamental work, "The Subsequent Sex," distributed in 1949. De Beauvoir's investigation of the social and existential states of ladies tested winning thoughts of orientation jobs. Her expressive study of male controlled society and her require ladies' freedom reverberated with women's activists around the world, laying the preparation for the women's activist developments of the twentieth 100 years.

The effect of words isn't restricted to the domain of the political or the socio-social; it stretches out to logical talk too. Albert Einstein's compositions, especially his hypothesis of relativity, upset how we might interpret the actual universe. While his papers might not have been discourses in the customary sense, their effect on logical idea and the public's impression of the universe has been amazing.

In the contemporary time, Malala Yousafzai's talks and works upholding for young ladies' schooling have caught the hearts and brains of individuals all over the planet. Malala's boldness, flexibility, and expressiveness, especially in her location to the Unified Countries in 2013, have made her a worldwide image of the battle for schooling and orientation balance. Her effect reaches out past the quick setting of her activism, moving people, everything being equal, to defend equity and schooling.

These authentic models altogether outline the different manners by which words can enthrall the majority, rising above social, semantic, and worldly limits. Whether conveyed in snapshots of political disturbance, social change, or individual contemplation, the effect of addresses and compositions lies in their capacity to bring out feelings, challenge points of view, and motivate activity. The getting through reverberation of these words highlights their immortal importance as impetuses for change, understanding, and aggregate advancement.

1.3 The psychological aspect of language and its influence on human emotions

The interchange among language and human feelings is a complicated and dynamic relationship that digs into the multifaceted functions of the human mind. Language, as a device for correspondence, has the exceptional capacity to pass data as well as on to shape, inspire, and mirror a wide range of feelings. The mental part of language envelops the manners by which words, articulations, and etymological subtleties impact human feelings, affecting discernments, perspectives, and relational connections.

Words hold the ability to inspire a scope of feelings, from euphoria and love to outrage and trouble. The decision of language, its tone, and the setting where it is utilized add to the close to home effect of correspondence. Positive and elevating words can move, inspire, and make a feeling of prosperity. On the other hand, the utilization of negative or brutal language can ingrain dread, tension, or hatred. Understanding the mental effect of language requires an investigation of phonetic components that add to close to home reactions.

One vital part of language that impacts feelings is the utilization of striking and reminiscent symbolism. Engaging and tangible rich language has the ability to make mental pictures that reverberate with people, setting off close to home reactions. Writers, for instance, utilize clear symbolism to inspire explicit sentiments and convey complex feelings. The force of engaging language lies in its capacity to ship people into the domain of creative mind, inspiring feelings that are profoundly associated with the tactile encounters it brings out.

Illustrations and analogies are phonetic gadgets that contribute essentially to the mental effect of language. By drawing equals and examinations, representations and likenesses give a method for communicating dynamic ideas in additional substantial terms. They tap into the mental and close to home spaces all the while, permitting people to get a handle on complex thoughts and experience related feelings. For example, depicting love as "an excursion" or "a fire" summons explicit close to home undertones that go past the exacting importance of the words.

The mood and rhythm of language likewise assume a urgent part in impacting feelings. The stream and pacing of discourse or composed text can make a feeling of congruity, fervor, or pressure. Think about the cadenced nature of verse or the conscious pacing of an inspirational discourse; both are intended to get close to home reactions by utilizing the intrinsic musicality of language. The profound reverberation of beat stretches out to regular discourse, where the rhythm and inflection can convey excitement, direness, or tranquility, forming the close to home tone of correspondence.

Notwithstanding the construction of language, the force of words to impact feelings is well established in their social and social settings. The implications and meanings joined to words are not static; they advance inside social systems and cultural standards. Certain words or articulations might convey social subtleties that bring out unambiguous close to home reactions in light of shared encounters, values, or verifiable settings. Understanding the social and social elements of language is urgent in getting a handle on its mental effect on feelings.

The idea of etymological relativity, frequently alluded to as the Sapir-Whorf speculation, places that the language we use shapes our impression of the world. The words accessible to us in a given language impact the manner in which we sort and decipher encounters. For instance, dialects that have explicit terms for nuanced feelings, like the Portuguese expression "saudade" or the Japanese idea of "mono no mindful," furnish people with an etymological structure to communicate and explore those feelings, molding their close to home scenes.

Language isn't just a device for communicating feelings yet in addition a method for managing and grasping them. The demonstration of really articulating sentiments, known as profound articulation, has restorative ramifications. Research in brain science proposes that articulating feelings verbally can add to profound prosperity by giving a feeling of clearness and command over one's inward encounters. The method involved with expressing feelings works with close to home guideline, permitting people to explore and figure out their sentiments.

Alternately, the concealment or aversion of profound articulation through language can negatively affect psychological well-being. At the point when people can't or reluctant to verbalize their feelings, it can prompt profound packaging, uplifted feelings of anxiety, and troubles in relational connections. The significance of language as a device for profound articulation highlights its job in encouraging mental prosperity and advancing capacity to understand people on a deeper level.

Past individual profound articulation, the social part of language adds to the arrangement of close to home bonds and the advancement of sympathy. Shared semantic encounters make a feeling of association and understanding among people, encouraging an aggregate capacity to understand individuals at their core inside networks. Discussions, narrating, and shared stories add to the social development of feelings, molding social standards and impacting how feelings are communicated and deciphered inside a general public.

The job of language in molding close to home reactions reaches out to non-verbal correspondence too. Looks, non-verbal communication, and manner of speaking act as non-verbal signs that supplement and improve the close to home substance of verbal correspondence. The arrangement of verbal and non-verbal signs adds to the generally speaking close to home effect of a message. Irregularities among verbal and non-verbal correspondence can prompt disarray or doubt, featuring the interconnected idea of language and feelings in relational cooperations.

The impact of language on feelings is additionally exemplified in the field of publicizing and promoting. Publicists fastidiously pick words, mottos, and visuals that inspire explicit close to home reactions to advance items or administrations. The convincing force of publicizing lies in its capacity to take advantage of shoppers' feelings, making relationship between a brand and certain sentiments. Whether it's the delight related with a specific soda or the feeling of experience connected to a movement objective, the language utilized in publicizing is painstakingly created to evoke wanted profound responses.

Besides, the effect of language on feelings has critical ramifications in the domain of influence and manner of speaking. Powerful correspondence includes the essential utilization of language to impact perspectives and ways of behaving. Aristotle's methods of influence — ethos, sentiment, and logos — feature the focal job of feelings (poignancy) in persuading a crowd of people. Viable influence frequently depends on the speaker's capacity to interface with the crowd inwardly, cultivating a feeling of sympathy and reverberation.

The outlining of messages is one more compelling part of language in the mental domain. How data is introduced, the selection of words, and the outlining of stories can shape the close to home reaction of the crowd. For example, outlining an issue as a danger as opposed to an open door can inspire dread and direness. Political talk, specifically, use outlining to shape public insights and evoke profound responses on issues going from migration to environmental change.

The effect of language on feelings isn't restricted to the expressed or composed word; it reaches out to self-talk and interior discourse. The accounts people develop inside their brains impact their profound encounters and self-insight. Positive self-talk, portrayed by insisting and empowering language, adds to a stronger and hopeful outlook. On the other hand, pessimistic self-talk, set apart by self-analysis and cruel language, can add to insecurities and nervousness.

Mental social treatment (CBT), a generally polished helpful methodology, perceives the significance of language in impacting feelings and ways of behaving. CBT underscores recognizing and testing negative idea examples and supplanting them with additional versatile and positive perspectives. This cycle, known as mental rebuilding, features the flexibility of feelings through changes in language and mental cycles.

The effect of language on close to home prosperity is especially clear in the field of psycholinguistics, which investigates the connection among language and discernment. Concentrates on in this field look at how language shapes mental cycles, including memory, consideration, and critical thinking. The etymological outlining of encounters can impact how people encode, recover, and decipher recollections, adding to the arrangement of close to home recollections and the advancement of mental blueprints.

1.4 Setting the stage for the journey to master the art of captivating audiences

Setting out on the excursion to excel at enthralling crowds includes a nuanced investigation of different components that add to compelling correspondence. This try reaches out past simple public talking or composing; it incorporates the capacity to draw in, move, and leave an enduring effect on different crowds. Making way for this excursion requires a comprehension of key standards, procedures, and the development of fundamental abilities that raise correspondence to a work of art.

At the center of spellbinding crowds lies the acknowledgment that viable correspondence is a two-way trade — an intuitive dance between the communicator and the crowd. It requires conveying a message as well as laying out an association that resounds with the audience members or perusers. The excursion starts with recognizing the crucial job of compassion in correspondence, where the capacity to comprehend and discuss the thoughts of others turns into a foundation of crowd commitment.

Sympathy, with regards to correspondence, includes the ability to see the viewpoints, feelings, and necessities of the crowd. It requires venturing into the shoes of the audience members or perusers, perceiving their interests, yearnings, and difficulties. By developing sympathy, communicators gain knowledge into the assumptions and receptivity of their crowd, empowering them to tailor their messages in manners that truly associate with the common human experience.

The excursion to dazzle crowds additionally includes sharpening the craft of narrating. Narrating is a strong vehicle for correspondence, rising above the limits of culture, language, and setting. Whether passed on through verbally expressed words, composed accounts, or visual mediums, stories can possibly summon feelings, encourage understanding, and make critical encounters. Narrating connects with the crowd on a profound level, making the substance appealing and thunderous.

A viable narrator comprehends the significance of making stories that have a reasonable construction, convincing characters, and a significant message. The force of narrating lies in the substance as well as in the conveyance. A talented narrator utilizes vocal regulation, pacing, and motions to improve the story, making a spellbinding encounter for the crowd. Through narrating, communicators can move their crowd to various universes, light their creative mind, and leave an enduring engraving on their brains.

The excursion to dazzle crowds is personally associated with the dominance of language. Words, picked insightfully and used with accuracy, become instruments of impact and reverberation. Language is a powerful instrument that reaches out past its strict significance; it conveys implications, social subtleties, and close to home weight.

Powerful communicators give fastidious consideration to the selection of words, guaranteeing that their language lines up with the tone, reason, and setting of their message.

A rich and differed jargon improves the informative weapons store, considering subtlety, nuance, and the capacity to convey complex thoughts. The authority of language includes persuasiveness as well as clearness. Communicators should find some kind of harmony among refinement and availability, fitting their language to the level of their crowd while keeping up with validness and profundity. The excursion to excel at enthralling crowds is, fundamentally, a consistent refinement of etymological abilities and an investigation of the unlimited conceivable outcomes of articulation.

In the computerized age, the excursion to enrapture crowds envelops the talented route of virtual spaces and online stages. The appearance of online entertainment, websites, webcasts, and video content has changed the scene of correspondence, introducing the two open doors and difficulties. Communicators should adjust to the developing elements of online commitment, where quickness, visual allure, and intuitiveness assume essential parts in catching and supporting crowd consideration.

Online entertainment, with its promptness and worldwide reach, requests an essential way to deal with content creation. The excursion includes becoming amazing at making compact and effective messages, using visuals to upgrade narrating, and utilizing the force of hashtags and patterns for perceivability. Understanding the calculations and elements of various stages becomes fundamental in augmenting the span and effect of online correspondence. The excursion to charm online crowds requires a sharp consciousness of computerized patterns, crowd inclinations, and the capacity to interface in a virtual scene genuinely.

Moreover, the excursion to spellbind crowds requires a pledge to nonstop personal growth. This includes looking for input, embracing productive analysis, and being available to gaining from the two victories and disappointments. The craft of charming crowds develops with the communicator's development, requiring versatility and an eagerness to refine one's methodology. Mindfulness assumes a vital part in this excursion, provoking communicators to ponder their assets, shortcomings, and regions for improvement.

Successful correspondence is certainly not a one-size-fits-all undertaking; it requires fitting the way to deal with the particular qualities and inclinations of the interest group. The excursion to enthrall crowds includes the craft of crowd examination — an inside and out comprehension of the socioeconomics, interests, and needs of those being tended to. Whether conveying to a different group, a specialty local area, or a particular segment, communicators should adjust their substance, language, and conveyance to line up with the assumptions and sensibilities of their crowd.

In the corporate domain, the excursion to dazzle crowds frequently meets with the craft of authority correspondence. Pioneers, whether tending to their groups, partners, or people in general, should encapsulate credibility, straightforwardness, and the capacity to motivate. The excursion includes fostering an initiative correspondence style that encourages trust, inspires activity, and lines up with the hierarchical culture. Viable pioneers perceive the effect of their words and activities on the confidence, efficiency, and commitment of their groups.

Public talking is a focal part of the excursion to charm crowds, requiring the development of powerful show abilities. The craft of public talking includes the verbal conveyance of a message as well as non-verbal components, for example, non-verbal communication, eye to eye connection, and signals. Public speakers should excel at stage presence, projecting certainty, and interfacing with the crowd. Strategies like explanatory gadgets, humor, and crowd connection add to the general effect of a show.

In the domain of composed correspondence, whether as articles, expositions, or books, the excursion to enamor crowds includes the specialty of piece. Scholars should focus on construction, intelligence, and the cunning utilization of language to compellingly pass on their message. The capacity to make a dazzling presentation, support commitment all through the substance, and leave an essential end is integral to the specialty of composing. Compelling authors additionally perceive the significance of altering and refining their work to accomplish clearness and effect.

Visual correspondence is a fundamental piece of the excursion to enthrall crowds, particularly in a period overwhelmed by mixed media content. The specialty of visual correspondence envelops visual communication, photography, videography, and the utilization of visual components in introductions. The essential combination of visuals improves narrating, supports key messages, and catches consideration. Communicators should foster a tasteful reasonableness and a comprehension of visual order to make convincing and significant visual substance.

The excursion to dazzle crowds converges with the domain of diversion, where entertainers, performers, and craftsmen draw in with their crowd through imagination and creative articulation. The craft of diversion includes specialized capability as well as the capacity to interface sincerely with the crowd. Entertainers should develop stage presence, mystique, and a genuine association that rises above the physical or virtual stage. The excursion in this space requires nonstop development, flexibility to crowd inclinations, and a guarantee to conveying critical encounters.

Morals and credibility are basic mainstays of the excursion to enrapture crowds. The specialty of correspondence is most powerful when grounded in truth, respectability, and a veritable association with the crowd.

Misleading strategies, manipulative procedures, or inauthentic personas can subvert the trust and validity fundamental for charming crowds. Communicators should explore the moral components of their specialty, guaranteeing that their messages line up with values, standards, and the prosperity of their crowd.

The excursion to become the best at enamoring crowds is innately connected to the capacity to explore difficulties and mishaps. Only one out of every odd endeavor will bring about absolute achievement, and communicators should be tough notwithstanding analysis or horrible results. The excursion includes gaining from disappointments, adjusting systems, and keeping a development mentality. Embracing difficulties as any open doors for learning adds to the refinement of abilities and the improvement of an informative versatility that braces the excursion.

Chapter 2

Crafting Compelling Content

Making convincing substance is a craftsmanship that requires a sensitive equilibrium of innovativeness, lucidity, and association. In the tremendous scene of composed correspondence, whether it be as articles, blog entries, or advertising materials, the capacity to connect with and charm a group of people is fundamental. In this investigation of content making, we'll dive into key components that add to the production of content that illuminates as well as reverberates with perusers on a significant level.

At the center of convincing substance lies a profound comprehension of the interest group. Prior to leaving on the excursion of creating content, it's basic to get a handle on the socioeconomics, inclinations, and trouble spots of the planned readership. This information fills in as the establishment whereupon any remaining components of content creation are fabricated. Whether the crowd is educated recent college grads or old pros, fitting the substance to suit their requirements and interests is pivotal.

Similarly significant is the foundation of a reasonable and convincing reason for the substance. Whether it plans to teach, engage, convince, or move, the general objective ought to be obvious all along. This clearness directs the substance maker as well as guarantees that the crowd can undoubtedly observe the worth they stand to acquire from concentrating on perusing.

The construction of the substance assumes a vital part in its viability. An efficient piece upgrades lucidness as well as works with the ingestion of data. The presentation ought to catch the peruser's eye, giving a brief look into the substance of the substance. The body of the substance ought to be legitimately organized, with each segment consistently changing into the following. At long last, the decision ought to have an enduring impression, summing up central issues and, if pertinent, offering a source of inspiration.

While structure gives the system, language fills in as the brushstroke that paints the material of content. The selection of words, tone, and style on the whole add to the general voice of the substance. Understanding the subtleties of language permits the substance maker to hit the right harmony with the crowd. Whether the goal is to convey authority, warmth, or humor, adjusting the language to the ideal tone is basic for successful correspondence.

In the computerized age, abilities to focus are momentary, making it pivotal to charm the crowd all along. The title fills in as the primary resource, and its job is similar to an alarm's call, enticing perusers to dive into the substance. Creating a convincing title includes a sensitive harmony among instruction and interest. It ought to give a brief look into the substance's quintessence while leaving enough inferred to provoke interest.

Past the title, the initial sentences of the substance are similarly indispensable. This is the represent the moment of truth second where the peruser chooses whether to proceed or continue on. A convincing opening might appear as a provocative inquiry, a strong statement, or an enthralling tale. Anything the methodology, it ought to lay out an association with the peruser and set the vibe for what follows.

In the domain of advanced content, visuals are strong partners in passing on data and upgrading commitment. Whether it be pictures, infographics, or recordings, visuals have the ability to convey complex ideas in an edible configuration. Coordinating pertinent visuals breaks the dullness of text as well as takes care of various learning styles, guaranteeing a more comprehensive and vivid experience for the crowd.

In any case, the joining of visuals ought to be deliberate and lined up with the substance's targets. Unessential or extreme utilization of visuals can degrade the message instead of upgrade it. Alt text for pictures is likewise significant for availability, guaranteeing that people with visual weaknesses can in any case understand the substance.

In the computerized scene, site design improvement (Website optimization) is a vital thought for content designers. The essential utilization of watchwords, meta depictions, and other Website optimization procedures can fundamentally influence a piece of content's perceivability on web crawlers. Notwithstanding, the specialty of creating convincing substance stretches out past basically taking care of calculations.

While Website design enhancement is a significant device for expanding discoverability, the core of content creation lies in its capacity to resound with human perusers. Realness is a foundation of convincing substance. Perusers can perceive when content is made exclusively for web crawlers, absent any and all authentic worth or significance. Finding some kind of harmony between Website design enhancement improvement and bona fide, significant substance is fundamental for supported commitment.

Commitment is a two-way road, and encouraging a feeling of local area around the substance can essentially intensify its effect. Empowering peruser collaboration through remarks, online entertainment offers, and conversations develops a feeling of having a place. This commitment expands the scope of the substance as well as gives significant bits of knowledge into the crowd's viewpoints and inclinations.

In a time where deception multiplies, the believability of content is of central significance. Laying out entrust with the crowd requires a guarantee to exactness, straightforwardness, and moral principles. Refering to dependable sources, truth really taking a look at data, and unveiling any likely irreconcilable circumstances add to the validity of the substance.

Besides, a predictable and credible voice constructs trust after some time. Perusers are bound to draw in with content that exudes a feeling of unwavering quality and honesty. This trust, once settled, turns into an important resource, cultivating a reliable readership that profits for quality substance.

Versatility is a sign of compelling substance creation. The scene of advanced correspondence is dynamic, with patterns, innovations, and crowd inclinations developing quickly. Effective substance makers stay receptive to these movements, embracing change and adjusting their systems in like manner.

One road through which versatility shows is in the investigation of assorted content configurations. While long-structure articles are powerful for inside and out investigation, more limited organizations, for example, blog entries, infographics, and recordings take care of differing crowd inclinations. Embracing interactive media content enhances the substance portfolio as well as extends its openness to various socioeconomics.

Notwithstanding design variety, keeping up to date with arising patterns and advances is significant. For example, the ascent of voice search has provoked a change in Web optimization procedures, with an emphasis on conversational and long-tail watchwords. Essentially, the coordination of man-made consciousness in satisfied creation presents additional opportunities for personalization and productivity.

Nonetheless, while flexibility is critical, remaining consistent with the center standards of viable communication is similarly significant. The basics of narrating, clearness, and crowd centricity stay immortal. Finding some kind of harmony among development and basic standards guarantees that content stays up with change as well as endures over the extreme long haul.

Content creation is a dynamic and iterative cycle. The excursion from the underlying plan to the last cleaned piece includes various phases of drafting, updating, and refining. Embracing this iterative nature takes into account constant improvement and refinement of the substance.

One powerful methodology is to look for criticism from friends, guides, or even the interest group during the drafting stages. New viewpoints can uncover vulnerable sides and proposition important experiences that add to the substance's improvement. Helpful analysis is an integral asset for development, and content makers ought to see it as a potential chance to refine their specialty.

Also, the joining of information driven experiences improves the iterative interaction. Breaking down measurements, for example, peruser commitment, skip rates, and virtual entertainment shares gives quantitative input on the substance's exhibition. This information driven approach empowers content makers to pursue informed choices and changes, guaranteeing that the substance stays lined up with crowd inclinations.

Chasing convincing substance, the craft of narrating becomes the overwhelming focus. Narrating rises above the simple movement of data; it winds around a story that resounds on a human level. Whether the substance is enlightening or special, implanting it with a convincing story catches the crowd's consideration and makes an essential encounter.

A very much created story follows a story curve, with a reasonable start, center, and end. The presentation sets the stage, presenting characters or ideas. The body unfurls the account, giving profundity and setting. The end integrates the components, having an enduring impression. Through narrating, even the most mind boggling or unremarkable points can be changed into connecting with and engaging substance.

In addition, narrating gives a close to home anchor to the crowd. Feelings are strong impetuses for memory and association. Content that evokes feeling, whether it be satisfaction, sympathy, or interest, lays out a more profound association with the crowd. This profound reverberation cultivates a feeling of appeal, making the substance more effective and critical.

While narrating is a strong instrument, the craft of straightforwardness ought to be considered carefully. Clear and brief correspondence is a sign of convincing substance. In a time where data over-burden is pervasive, curtness is an ideals. Each word ought to fill a need, adding to the general clearness and effect of the message.

Staying away from language and pointless intricacy guarantees that the substance is open to a more extensive crowd. The objective isn't to dazzle with phonetic tumbling however to convey thoughts in a way that is handily perceived. Straight-forwardness in articulation doesn't decrease the refinement of thought; rather.

2.1 Understanding your audience: demographics, interests, and prefer-ences

Understanding your crowd is a foundation of compelling correspondence, and in the domain of content creation, a central perspective can shape the achievement or disappointment of your undertakings. At the core of this figuring out lies an exhaustive handle of your crowd's socioeconomics, interests, and inclinations. This information fills in as the compass directing the making of content that reverber-ates, draws in, and adds authentic worth.

Socioeconomics structure the bedrock of crowd understanding. These are the quantitative properties that characterize a gathering. Age, orientation, area, pay level, training, and occupation are normal segment factors. Gathering and examining this information gives a depiction of the qualities that characterize your crowd. Whether you are tending to an energetic, educated segment or a more developed and monetarily laid out bunch, fitting your substance to line up with these segment subtleties is fundamental.

The age of your crowd can impact not just the language and tone of your substance yet in addition the selection of points and the favored substance design. For example, more youthful crowds could answer all the more well to outwardly captivating substance like recordings and infographics, while more seasoned crowds could see the value in top to bottom articles or whitepapers.

Orientation is another basic segment factor that can shape the tone, symbolism, and topics of your substance. Understanding the particular interests and worries of various sexual orientations permits you to make content that feels important and engaging. Furthermore, taking into account the different points of view inside orientation bunches guarantees a more comprehensive way to deal with content creation.

Geographic area is a critical determinant of social impacts, language inclinations, and even time regions. Content that reverberates in one area might not have a similar effect in another. Adjusting your substance to line up with the social setting of your crowd's area shows a nuanced grasping that improves commitment.

Pay level and training give experiences into the financial status of your crowd. This data can direct choices on the intricacy of language utilized, the profundity of examination introduced, and, surprisingly, the kinds of items or administrations highlighted in your substance. Fitting your informing to line up with the financial and instructive profile of your crowd improves importance and appeal.

Occupation is a segment factor that can impact the expert setting in which your crowd draws in with content. Whether your crowd comprises of experts in money, medical services, or innovation, adjusting your substance to their industry-explicit interests and difficulties guarantees that it enhances their expert lives.

Past socioeconomics, digging into the interests of your crowd gives a more nuanced comprehension of their inclinations and inspirations. Interests include a wide range, going from side interests and sporting exercises to proficient pursuits and self-improvement. Distinguishing and lining up with these interests permits you to make content that catches consideration and cultivates a feeling of association.

One way to deal with uncovering crowd interests is to investigate information from different touchpoints, for example, site examination, online entertainment commitment, and client reviews. These sources give significant bits of knowledge into the points, topics, and sorts of content that resound most with your crowd. Moreover, observing industry drifts and remaining receptive to mainstream society permits you to expect to develop interests and designer your substance technique as needs be.

Understanding the inclinations of your crowd goes past satisfied subjects to incorporate the arrangement, tone, and style that resound most with them. A few crowds might favor succinct and outwardly engaging substance, while others might incline towards inside and out, information driven investigation. Trying different things with various substance organizations and checking crowd reaction distinguishes the inclinations that adjust most intimately with your main interest group.

Web-based entertainment stages are integral assets for measuring crowd inclinations. Examining measurements like likes, offers, and remarks gives constant input on the substance that resounds most with your crowd. Also, observing commitment measurements on your site, for example, time spent on pages and skip rates, offers important bits of knowledge into the viability of your substance in catching and keeping up with crowd consideration.

In the advanced age, the significance of personalization couldn't possibly be more significant. Crowd fragments are different, and a one-size-fits-all way to deal with content creation is frequently inadequate. Utilizing innovation to carry out personalization techniques improves the importance of your substance and cultivates a more customized client experience.

Personalization can take different structures, from fitting substance suggestions in view of client conduct to powerfully changing the substance showed in light of client inclinations. Email promoting efforts that address beneficiaries by name and give customized suggestions are instances of how personalization can be carried out to make a more individualized association with the crowd.

Understanding your crowd is a continuous interaction that requires persistent observing and transformation. As crowd inclinations develop and recent fads arise, remaining receptive to these movements guarantees that your substance stays pertinent and resounding. Routinely returning to crowd socioeconomics, interests, and inclinations permits you to refine your substance procedure and settle on informed choices that line up with the powerful idea of your crowd.

One successful technique for social affair crowd experiences is using studies and criticism components. Straightforwardly looking for input from your crowd on their inclinations, difficulties, and assumptions gives an abundance of subjective information that supplements quantitative examination. Studies can be directed through different channels, including email, virtual entertainment, or inserted on your site.

Drawing in with your crowd progressively through live occasions, online classes, or web-based entertainment visits offers an intuitive stage for grasping their requirements and inclinations. The immediate trade of thoughts considers a more profound association and gives prompt input that can illuminate your substance system. This commitment likewise refines your image, encouraging a feeling of local area and dependability among your crowd.

Social listening is a significant device for acquiring experiences into crowd feeling and conversations encompassing your image or industry. Checking virtual entertainment stages and online gatherings permits you to recognize arising patterns, address concerns, and measure the general impression of your image. This ongoing input circle upgrades your capacity to answer crowd necessities and assumptions.

In the mission to comprehend your crowd, sympathy is a core value. Sympathy includes putting yourself in the shoes of your crowd, figuring out their difficulties, yearnings, and viewpoints. This sympathetic methodology illuminates the tone, informing, and content subjects, making an association that goes past conditional commitment.

Making purchaser personas is a functional methodology for exemplifying crowd compassion. Purchaser personas are point by point, semi-fictitious portrayals of your ideal clients in view of genuine information and taught hypothesis. Creating personas permits you to adapt your crowd, making it more straightforward to fit your substance to address their particular requirements and interests.

With regards to B2B (business-to-business) promoting, understanding your crowd stretches out to perceiving the different partners engaged with the dynamic interaction. A B2B buy choice frequently includes various people with particular jobs, obligations, and needs. Fitting substance to address the worries and interests of every partner improves the probability of fruitful commitment and transformation.

Openness is a critical thought in crowd understanding. Guaranteeing that your substance is available to people with handicaps widens its scope and inclusivity. This incorporates giving elective text to pictures, utilizing decipherable textual styles and variety differences, and planning an easy to understand site interface. Openness lines up with the standards of variety and consideration, mirroring a guarantee to coming to and serving a different crowd.

2.2 Identifying key messages and themes

Distinguishing key messages and subjects is a significant stage in the substance creation process, giving a firm structure that directs the turn of events and correspondence of data. Whether creating a blog entry, promoting effort, or a whole brand story, the clearness and reverberation of key messages assume a urgent part in catching crowd consideration and conveying the expected significance.

At its quintessence, key informing includes refining the center thoughts, values, and recommendations that you need to impart to your crowd. These messages act as the anchor focuses around which your substance rotates, giving a bound together and centered story. To actually distinguish key messages, it's fundamental to dive into the center parts of your image, item, or content targets.

One fundamental component of distinguishing key messages is a far reaching comprehension of your image or content's special incentive. What separates your image? What worth does your item or content propose to your crowd? Explaining these viewpoints characterizes the overall subjects that will resound with your interest group. It's not simply about what you need to say at the same time, more significantly, about what your crowd needs to hear.

Consider the trouble spots or difficulties that your crowd faces. Key messages ought to straightforwardly address these worries, offering arrangements or experiences that line up with your image's goals. Understanding your crowd's necessities permits you to tailor messages that catch consideration as well as offer significant benefit, making an association that goes past shallow correspondence.

Also, key messages ought to line up with your image's character and values. Consistency in informing cultivates brand honesty and assembles entrust with your crowd. Assuming your image underlines advancement, your key messages ought to mirror this obligation to state of the art arrangements. On the off chance that social obligation is a fundamental belief, your messages ought to pass on a feeling of direction and moral commitment. The arrangement between key messages and brand character fortifies the validness of your correspondence.

With regards to content creation, the recognizable proof of key subjects is firmly interlaced with key messages. Topics act as overall ideas or thoughts that go through your substance, binding together its different components.

These subjects might be account driven, zeroing in on narrating to pass on messages, or they can be more unique, like featuring explicit feelings or encounters.

One powerful technique in recognizing key subjects is to consider the bigger account you need to convey. Is it safe to say that you are recounting an account of beating difficulties, development, or change? The focal subject ought to reverberate with your crowd, making a paramount and significant experience. The selection of subjects ought to line up with the close to home and scholarly reaction you mean to summon in your crowd.

An exhaustive examination of your crowd's inclinations, perspectives, and ways of behaving is instrumental in forming key messages and subjects. Instruments, for example, crowd reviews, web-based entertainment examination, and statistical surveying give significant experiences into the outlook of your objective segment. By understanding what resounds with your crowd, you can fit messages and subjects to live up to their assumptions and inclinations.

Contender investigation is one more significant part of the message and subject ID process. By understanding how your rivals convey their messages and the subjects they underscore, you can recognize holes or chances to separate your image. This examination helps in making messages that hang out in the packed computerized scene, reverberating all the more successfully with your ideal interest group.

The method involved with distinguishing key messages and subjects is definitely not a one-time try. It requires nonstop refinement and variation, particularly in light of changes on the lookout, crowd elements, or industry patterns. Routinely returning to and reconsidering your key messages guarantees that they stay pertinent, thunderous, and lined up with your general goals.

One compelling technique for refining key messages is through A/B testing. This includes introducing various forms of your messages or content to fragments of your crowd and dissecting their reactions. By contrasting the presentation of various messages, you can accumulate information on what reverberates most successfully with your crowd. This iterative methodology permits you to advance your messages in light of ongoing criticism.

In the advanced age, where capacities to focus are restricted, the brevity of key messages is central. Creating brief messages that slice through the commotion and catch consideration is a workmanship. The "short presentation" idea, which includes articulating your critical messages in the time it takes a lift to go between floors, highlights the significance of curtness and clearness.

Each key message ought to be created with the "Three Cs" at the top of the priority list: lucidity, cognizance, and consistency. Lucidity guarantees that your message is handily grasped, keeping away from equivocalness or disarray.

Rationality guarantees that your messages structure a strong account, adding to a brought together brand story. Consistency guarantees that your messages adjust across different touchpoints, building up the all-encompassing topics.

The force of narrating is a vital component in passing on key messages and topics really. People are wired to interface with stories, and consolidating narrating into your substance makes a convincing and essential experience. Whether sharing client examples of overcoming adversity, brand beginning stories, or contextual investigations, narrating gives a vehicle to your critical messages to resound genuinely with your crowd.

The account construction of narrating ordinarily includes a start, center, and end. The start presents the setting, characters, and setting. The center unfurls the difficulties or excursion, giving profundity and setting to your messages. The end integrates the components, having an enduring impression. This design permits your vital messages to be woven consistently into a story that enthralls your crowd.

Visual components assume a vital part in supporting key messages and topics. Whether through pictures, infographics, or recordings, visuals have the ability to improve the profound effect of your messages and make them more critical. The selection of varieties, symbolism, and plan components ought to line up with the subjects you need to convey, making a strong visual language that builds up your messages.

Also, consistency in visual components adds to memorability. At the point when your crowd experiences steady obvious signs across different stages, it supports the commonality and trust related with your image. This consistency reaches out to the utilization of logos, text styles, and other plan components that add to the generally speaking visual character of your messages.

With regards to promoting and brand correspondence, the utilization of mottos or slogans is a strong device for typifying key messages. A very much created trademark distils the quintessence of your image or mission into a brief and significant expression. The Nike trademark, "Do what needs to be done," is an exemplary illustration of a slogan that exemplifies the brand's ethos and reverberates with its crowd.

While making trademarks or slogans, it's fundamental to guarantee that they line up with the qualities and subjects of your image. A noteworthy slogan can turn into a revitalizing sob for your crowd, connecting a strong opinion with your image. Whether rousing, persuasive, or funny, the tone of your slogan ought to be harmonious with your vital messages and the close to home reaction you expect to bring out.

Web-based entertainment stages are dynamic fields for passing on key messages and subjects. The succinct idea of online entertainment correspondence requests an engaged and effective way to deal with informing.

Hashtags, for example, can be utilized decisively to support key subjects and make a brought together discussion around your image or mission. Web-based entertainment examination give constant bits of knowledge into crowd responses, permitting you to refine your messages in view of client commitment.

In the time of content immersion, making a profound association with your crowd is a strong technique for guaranteeing that your key messages resound. Feelings have the ability to fashion enduring recollections and impact independent direction. Whether summoning euphoria, sympathy, energy, or wistfulness, the close to home tone of your messages adds to the general effect of your correspondence.

Understanding the close to home triggers that resound with your crowd requires a nuanced comprehension of their inspirations and goals. Leading crowd studies or investigating online entertainment feeling can give experiences into the profound reactions that particular subjects or messages evoke. Creating messages that tap into these close to home resonances upgrades the appeal and memorability of your substance.

A fundamental part of recognizing key messages and subjects is guaranteeing that they are versatile to various stages and mediums. Your crowd draws in with content across a different scope of channels, from online entertainment and websites to digital recordings and recordings. Fitting your messages to suit the novel qualities of every stage guarantees that your substance stays powerful and full.

Multichannel consistency includes adjusting the configuration of your messages as well as keeping a strong story across different touchpoints. Whether a client experiences your image on Instagram, your site, or a digital broadcast, the fundamental subjects and messages ought to adjust, adding to a bound together and conspicuous brand character.

Examination and information driven experiences are important devices in surveying the adequacy of your critical messages and topics. Observing measurements, for example, commitment rates, navigate rates, and change rates gives quantitative criticism on the effect of your messages. A/B testing, referenced prior, is one strategy.

2.3 The art of storytelling: creating narratives that resonate

The specialty of narrating is an immortal and strong type of correspondence that rises above societies, ages, and mediums. From old oral customs to contemporary computerized stages, stories have been a basic method for passing on data, bestowing shrewdness, and cultivating profound associations. In the domain of content creation, becoming the best at narrating is fundamental for making stories that resound with crowds on a significant level.

At its center, narrating includes creating stories that unfurl over the long haul, connecting with the crowd's creative mind, feelings, and keenness. A very much recounted story has the ability to charm consideration, bring out compassion, and leave an enduring effect. Whether in writing, film, advertising, or regular discussion, the standards of narrating stay steady, enveloping components like plot, characters, setting, and subject.

The principal mainstay of compelling narrating is the plot — the grouping of occasions that structure the story structure. A convincing plot presents struggle, fabricates strain, and resolves in a fantastic way. It takes the crowd on an excursion, holding their consideration through the expectation of what will occur straightaway. Whether a straightforward tale or an unpredictable adventure, a very much created plot is the foundation of any captivating story.

The design of a story ordinarily follows a three-act worldview: the arrangement, conflict, and goal. The arrangement presents the characters, setting, and starting conditions. The showdown presents difficulties, clashes, and rising activity that impel the story forward. The goal brings conclusion, tending to the contentions and giving a feeling of satisfaction. This design, frequently alluded to as the legend's excursion, reverberates with crowds across different societies and narrating customs.

Characters reinvigorate a story, filling in as the courses through which the crowd draws in with the story. Whether heroes, adversaries, or supporting characters, their inspirations, defects, and changes shape the close to home bend of the story. Creating engaging and dynamic characters permits the crowd to put resources into their excursions, producing a more profound association with the story.

Successful person advancement includes conveying the outside credits as well as the unseen conflicts and development. Defective characters with engaging difficulties frequently reverberate all the more firmly with crowds, as they reflect the intricacies of genuine encounters. The crowd's capacity to feel for the characters shapes an extension among fiction and reality, improving the profound effect of the story.

Setting lays out the scenery against which the story unfurls. It incorporates actual areas as well as the social, authentic, and cultural settings that shape the characters and occasions. A strikingly portrayed setting gives extravagance and profundity to the story, drenching the crowd in a world that feels substantial and legitimate. Whether a fantastical domain, a verifiable period, or a contemporary cityscape, the setting adds to the general environment and state of mind of the story.

Topics structure the basic messages, thoughts, or ethics inserted inside the story. They act as the core values that give the account profundity and reverberation. Subjects can investigate general ideas like love, mental fortitude, and recovery, or address more unambiguous issues

pertinent to the setting of the story. The investigation of subjects permits the crowd to get importance and importance from the story, hoisting it past simple diversion.

The specialty of narrating stretches out past the conventional domains of writing and film into the area of advertising and brand correspondence. In the business world, narrating is an amazing asset for conveying brand character, values, and contributions in a convincing and paramount way. Brands that become amazing at narrating make accounts that feature their items or administrations as well as reverberate with the feelings and desires of their ideal interest group.

One critical part of brand narrating is laying out a brand story — a firm and predictable story that conveys the brand's substance. This account frequently incorporates the brand's history, fundamental beliefs, and the interesting incentive it offers. Through brand narrating, organizations can refine their character, encouraging an association with customers that goes past conditional connections.

With regards to showcasing, the client venture turns into a story curve. From the underlying mindfulness stage to the last buy or commitment, each touchpoint adds to the unfurling story of the client's cooperation with the brand. Making a consistent and drawing in client venture story includes understanding the crowd's necessities, tending to trouble spots, and directing them toward a goal that lines up with the brand's targets.

The reconciliation of narrating in promoting reaches out to content creation across different stages, including sites, virtual entertainment, and publicizing. Web-based entertainment stages, specifically, give a powerful space to brands to share stories progressively, utilizing the instantaneousness and intuitiveness of these channels. Brands can utilize narrating to make interesting and shareable substance, cultivating a feeling of local area and commitment.

Besides, narrating in promoting isn't bound to text based content; visuals assume a vital part. The utilization of pictures, recordings, and infographics permits brands to pass on stories in an outwardly convincing way. Visual narrating has the ability to inspire feelings, improve on complex ideas, and have an enduring impression. The decision of visuals ought to line up with the brand story, building up key messages and subjects.

In the computerized age, where data is plentiful, capacities to focus are brief, and contest for crowd commitment is extraordinary, the standards of narrating become considerably more basic. The idea of "transmedia narrating" includes broadening a story across numerous media stages to make a firm and vivid experience. Brands can use this way to deal with draw in crowds across different channels, giving an all encompassing and interconnected story.

Integrating client produced content into the brand account is one more powerful technique in the computerized scene. Empowering clients to share their encounters, tributes, and stories connected with the brand makes a credible and engaging aspect to the account. Client created content upgrades brand validity as well as cultivates a feeling of local area among clients.

The idea of narrating isn't elite to outside correspondence; it assumes a critical part in inner correspondence inside associations. Inside narrating includes conveying the organization's main goal, values, and objectives to workers in a convincing and open way. Through stories that feature accomplishments, challenges, and the aggregate excursion, associations can cultivate a feeling of mutual perspective and responsibility among their groups.

Initiative narrating is a subset of inner narrating that includes pioneers speaking with realness and straightforwardness. Sharing individual tales, examples learned, and the vision for what's in store makes an association among pioneers and colleagues. This type of narrating rouses as well as supports a positive hierarchical culture.

The specialty of narrating isn't bound to prearranged accounts; it reaches out to unconstrained and conversational narrating in ordinary correspondence. Whether in private discussions, introductions, or public talking, the capacity to express thoughts through narrating upgrades the effect of the message. Stories, illustrations, and models drawn from individual encounters make a significant and engaging correspondence style.

Public speakers frequently utilize narrating methods to draw in and associate with their crowd. Opening a show with a convincing story catches consideration and lays out an association all along. Integrating accounts to represent central issues, pass on information, or present contextual investigations makes the data more available and important. The utilization of narrating openly talking changes data into a durable and significant story.

Instructive settings benefit essentially from the coordination of narrating. Instructors who integrate stories into their illustrations make a really captivating and paramount opportunity for growth. Whether showing history, science, or writing, meshing stories into the educational program gives setting, significance, and a more profound comprehension of the topic. The story way to deal with training rises above age gatherings and learning conditions, encouraging an adoration for learning.

The crossing point of narrating and innovation has led to new and vivid narrating designs. Computer generated reality (VR), increased reality (AR), and intelligent narrating encounters offer crowds phenomenal degrees of commitment. These advances permit clients to step into the account, interface with characters, and impact the story's result. The development of innovation keeps on opening new boondocks for narrating, extending its prospects and effect.

Notwithstanding the different utilizations of narrating across different spaces, the center rules that make a story convincing stay reliable. Realness is a key part in compelling narrating. Whether passing on a brand story, a showcasing message, or an individual tale, validness makes a veritable association with the crowd. Real narrating includes being consistent with the brand's qualities, the speaker's voice, or the embodiment of the account.

Profound reverberation is one more key component of powerful narrating. Stories that bring out feelings — whether bliss, compassion, shock, or motivation — leave an enduring effect. Feelings have the ability to make a paramount encounter and impact the crowd's discernment and conduct. Making stories that tap into the close to home scene of the crowd upgrades their association with the story.

The idea of the "story curve" is principal to making accounts that reverberate. A very much organized story circular segment includes a presentation, rising activity, peak, falling activity, and goal. This bend makes an ability to stay on beat and force, directing the crowd through a convincing excursion. Whether in a novel, a film, or a promoting effort, a painstakingly created story curve holds the crowd's consideration and leaves them with a feeling of satisfaction.

The utilization of tension and strain adds a component of interest to narrating. Whether through startling unexpected developments, unsettled clashes, or a steady disclosure of data, keeping a degree of tension enthralls the crowd's consideration. The expectation of what will occur next keeps the crowd drew in and put resources into the unfurling story.

The force of narrating lies in what is said as well as in what is left implied. The specialty of suggestion and idea permits the crowd to fill in the holes with their creative mind. Leaving space for understanding welcomes the crowd to become dynamic members in the narrating system, making a more vivid and customized insight.

The idea of the "legend's excursion," promoted by Joseph Campbell, is a general narrating original that reverberates across societies and sorts. The legend's process includes a hero who leaves on an experience, faces difficulties, goes through change, and returns changed. This model gives a format to stories that investigate development, strength, and the victory of the human soul.

The craft of narrating likewise includes the talented utilization of language. Whether spoken or composed, the selection of words, allegories, and symbolism adds to the general effect of the account. Distinct language makes a clear mental picture, permitting the crowd to drench themselves in the story. The beat and rhythm of the language add a musicality that upgrades the narrating experience.

With regards to mark narrating, the brand voice is a urgent component of language. The brand voice envelops the tone, style, and character of the brand's correspondence. Whether conveying a comical inclination, authority, or sympathy, the consistency of the brand voice across different touchpoints makes a firm and unmistakable personality.

In the computerized time, where consideration is a valuable product and data is bountiful, the craft of narrating remains as a reference point. In an ocean of content, stories have the ability to slice through the commotion and make a significant association. Whether through a painstakingly created promoting effort, an effective brand story, or a convincing individual story, the specialty of narrating proceeds to shape and enhance the manner in which we convey, interface, and figure out the world.

2.4 Balancing information and entertainment to maintain engagement

Adjusting data and diversion is a fragile and fundamental craftsmanship in the domain of content creation. During a time where capacities to focus are transient and a wealth of data strives for crowd commitment, the combination of enlightening substance with engaging components becomes significant. Whether in promoting, instructive undertakings, or narrating, the amicable mix of data and amusement is the way to catching and keeping up with the crowd's consideration.

At the core of this fragile equilibrium is the acknowledgment that individuals draw in with content for different reasons. A look for significant data to address a particular need or inquiry, while others are attracted to content that engages and gives a break from schedule. The test for content makers is to take care of both these requirements all the while, guaranteeing that useful substance is introduced in a drawing in and engaging way.

One central standard in adjusting data and amusement is to completely figure out the interest group. Perceiving the socioeconomics, inclinations, and ways of behaving of the crowd illuminates content makers about the best ways of conveying data while keeping the substance engaging. A nuanced comprehension of the crowd's inspirations takes into consideration the production of content that reverberates on an individual level.

With regards to instructive substance, keeping up with commitment is many times a test as conventional learning materials can be seen as dry and unsuitable. By mixing instructive substance with engaging components, teachers can make the opportunity for growth more charming and essential. Instructive games, intuitive reproductions, and narrating methods are successful systems to adjust the conveyance of data with amusement in instructive settings.

In promoting, where the goal is to pass on data about items or administrations, the test is to introduce this data in a manner that spellbinds and holds the crowd's advantage. Narrating, humor, and convincing visuals are devices in the advertiser's weapons store to implant diversion

into the educational parts of a mission. Fruitful promoting efforts frequently influence stories that draw in feelings and make an essential effect.

The idea of infotainment, a portmanteau of data and diversion, typifies the possibility of flawlessly mixing genuine substance with engaging components. Infotainment looks to teach and illuminate while keeping the crowd engaged. Whether in the configuration of network shows, online recordings, or intelligent encounters, infotainment has shown to be an effective methodology for keeping up with commitment.

The harmony among data and diversion is exemplified in the realm of newscasting. Media sources, confronted with the test of introducing frequently complicated and serious data, consolidate narrating methods, visuals, and drawing in arrangements to keep their crowd educated and intrigued. The appearance of computerized reporting has delivered additional opportunities for media narrating, permitting news associations to pass on data in convincing and intelligent ways.

One way to deal with adjusting data and amusement is the utilization of account narrating. Narrating has an intrinsic diversion esteem, drawing on the well established custom of stories that catch the creative mind. Whether in composed articles, video content, or promoting efforts, the utilization of narrating methods changes data into a firm and drawing in story. By introducing data inside a story structure, content makers give setting, profound reverberation, and a feeling of movement that keeps the crowd snared.

Visual components assume an essential part in adjusting data and diversion. The human cerebrum processes visual data more productively than text, making visuals a powerful device for passing on data in a drawing in way. Infographics, recordings, livelinesss, and intelligent illustrations are designs that influence the force of visuals to work on complex ideas and keep up with crowd interest.

In the domain of web-based entertainment, where content seeks consideration in a quick looking over climate, visuals become significantly more pivotal. Eye-getting pictures, connecting with recordings, and stylishly satisfying plans are bound to stop the parchment and catch the crowd's consideration. Virtual entertainment stages additionally offer elements like stories, merry go rounds, and live recordings that give dynamic and engaging ways of sharing data.

Humor is a powerful instrument for mixing diversion into content without settling on the conveyance of data. Whether in composed content, recordings, or showcasing efforts, humor makes a positive and pleasant experience for the crowd. It eases up the tone as well as makes the substance more engaging and paramount. Nonetheless, it's fundamental to be aware of the specific situation and crowd to guarantee that humor lines up with the general informing.

Intuitive substance is one more procedure for adjusting data and diversion. Intelligent components, for example, tests, surveys, and games, welcome crowd support and commitment. This makes the substance more agreeable as well as gives important experiences into crowd inclinations and ways of behaving. Intelligent substance diverts the crowd from uninvolved customers into dynamic members, cultivating a feeling of inclusion.

The idea of gamification takes intelligent substance to a higher level by integrating game-like components into non-game settings. Whether in schooling, representative preparation, or showcasing, gamification adds a serious and engaging layer to the conveyance of data. Focuses, rewards, and difficulties rouse the crowd to draw in with the substance and progress through the material in a more pleasant way.

Digital recordings have arisen as a well known medium that flawlessly mixes data and diversion. Webcasts cover a large number of points, from genuine wrongdoing and history to science and self improvement. The conversational and narrating nature of web recordings permits hosts to pass on data in a loose and engaging way. The closeness of the sound configuration frequently makes an association among hosts and audience members, making the learning or enlightening experience more charming.

Live streaming is a powerful type of content creation that carries instantaneousness and intelligence to the crowd. Whether utilized for instructive purposes, item exhibits, or in the background glimpses, live streaming connects with the crowd progressively. Watchers can clarify some pressing issues, take part in conversations, and feel a feeling of association with the substance maker. The live and unscripted nature of live streaming frequently adds an engaging component.

The harmony among data and diversion stretches out to the composed word. Blog entries, articles, and long-structure content can be made in a manner that teaches and illuminates while keeping the peruser locked in. The utilization of narrating strategies, conversational tone, and an outwardly engaging design adds to the general peruser experience. Well-informed and educational substance can be introduced in a configuration that is open, pleasant, and helpful for supported commitment.

With regards to long-shape composed content, breaking data into absorbable areas with subheadings, list items, and visuals upgrades meaningfulness. This approach obliges different understanding inclinations and urges the crowd to investigate the substance at their own speed. The essential utilization of arranging components adds to the general stream and commitment of the composed material.

The idea of edutainment, a combination of instruction and diversion, epitomizes the deliberate mixing of these two components. Edutainment tries to teach the crowd in an engaging and agreeable way.

Instructive TV projects, narratives, and intelligent displays in exhibition halls are instances of edutainment. The goal is to make learning a pleasurable encounter, encouraging interest and commitment.

While making content that adjusts data and amusement, taking into account the pacing of the material is critical. A very much paced show of data keeps up with the crowd's advantage all through the substance. This includes staying away from data over-burden, differentiating the arrangement of content, and consolidating snapshots of commitment, for example, tests or reflections, to separate the stream and keep the crowd mindful.

The idea of the "diversion esteem" of content addresses its capacity to dazzle, entertain, or draw in the crowd. Content makers frequently evaluate the amusement worth of their material by considering variables, for example, narrating quality, visual allure, and the general experience it gives. While the essential objective might be to pass on data, guaranteeing that the substance has diversion esteem upgrades its viability.

The joining of innovation, for example, man-made brainpower and augmented reality, opens additional opportunities for making vivid and engaging encounters. Computer generated reality, specifically, permits clients to step into mimicked conditions, giving a degree of commitment that rises above customary substance designs. The utilization of vivid innovations adds to a more intelligent and vital learning or educational experience.

The iterative idea of content creation includes nonstop assessment and transformation in light of crowd criticism and examination. Checking measurements, for example, commitment rates, navigate rates, and time spent on satisfied gives experiences into what perspectives are resounding with the crowd. Examining this information permits content makers to refine their methodology, streamlining the harmony among data and diversion.

Chapter 3

Mastering the Art of Persuasion

In the tremendous domain of human communication, the capacity to convince is an expertise that rises above callings, societies, and social settings. Whether you are a sales rep planning to finalize a negotiation, a pioneer motivating a group, or a singular trying to influence feelings, excelling at influence is a urgent resource. It is the unpretentious dance of words, signals, and feelings that can change the tides in support of yourself and shape the course of discussions and choices.

At its center, influence isn't about control or pressure however about impacting others enthusiastically and morally. It is the specialty of making convincing accounts, building trust, and figuring out the brain science of your crowd. To really turn into an expert of influence, one should dive into the complexities of human way of behaving, correspondence elements, and the force of sympathy.

The underpinning of powerful correspondence lies in the specialty of undivided attention. Prior to endeavoring to convince others, one must initially figure out their viewpoints, concerns, and inspirations. Undivided attention goes past hearing words; it includes sympathetic grasping, recognizing feelings, and showing authentic interest in what others need to say. At the point when individuals feel appreciated and esteemed, they are bound to be responsive to your thoughts.

One more foundation of compelling influence is laying out validity. Individuals are normally disposed to stand by listening to those they see as educated, reliable, and genuine. Building believability requires a blend of skill, uprightness, and reliable correspondence. Exhibiting capability in your field, being straightforward about your goals, and keeping a history of dependability all add to upgrading your validity as a convincing communicator.

Making an influential message includes what you say as well as how you say it. The force of language, tone, and non-verbal communication couldn't possibly be more significant. Words can inspire feelings, make mental pictures, and impact insights. A very much created message thinks about the crowd's qualities, feelings, and mental predispositions, fitting the substance to resound with their one of a kind points of view.

Tone, as well, assumes a significant part in influence. The manner in which you convey a message can either welcome cooperation or impel opposition. A positive and conscious tone cultivates receptiveness and receptivity, while a fierce or pompous tone can prompt protectiveness and resistance. Understanding the subtleties of tone and changing it in view of the specific situation and crowd is an expertise that recognizes an enticing communicator.

Similarly significant is the non-verbal part of correspondence. Non-verbal communication, looks, and signals convey unobtrusive prompts that can either support or go against verbal messages. Keeping in touch, taking on open and certain stances, and reflecting the non-verbal communication of others can improve your convincing effect. Consistency among verbal and non-verbal signs fabricates trust and supports the genuineness of your message.

Influence is certainly not a one-size-fits-all undertaking. Various people have shifting correspondence styles, inclinations, and dynamic cycles. Fitting your way to deal with match the novel qualities of your crowd is a vital part of fruitful influence. This requires versatility, compassion, and the capacity to really peruse expressive gestures.

Understanding the mental triggers that impact navigation is a powerful device in the weapons store of an enticing communicator. The rule of correspondence, wherein people feel a sense of urgency to return some help, can be utilized to make an awareness of others' expectations. Offering esteem, whether as data, help, or veritable concern, lays out an equal powerful that improves the probability of collaboration.

Moreover, the idea of social evidence features the effect of friend impact on independent direction. Individuals are more disposed to embrace a specific way of behaving or conviction in the event that they see others in their group of friends doing likewise. Using tributes, contextual investigations, or instances of agreement inside a local area can enhance the powerful impact by taking advantage of the human tendency to line up with the apparent larger part.

The shortage standard is one more mental trigger that can be bridled for convincing purposes. Individuals will generally appoint higher worth to things that are seen as uncommon or in restricted supply. Making a feeling of shortage, whether through selective offers, restricted time advancements, or stressing the uniqueness of a recommendation, can upgrade its engaging quality and earnestness.

Correspondence, social confirmation, and shortage are only a couple of instances of the mental standards supporting influential correspondence. Understanding these standards gives a system to creating messages that reverberate with the inborn inclinations of human discernment and conduct. Notwithstanding, moral contemplations should direct the utilization of such standards to guarantee that influence stays a power for positive impact as opposed to control.

In the domain of influence, narrating arises as a strong device for drawing in feelings and conveying complex thoughts. People are innately attracted to stories that resound with their encounters, goals, and values. A very much recounted story has the ability to make an association, summon sympathy, and have an enduring impression.

The specialty of narrating includes the actual account as well as the essential utilization of pacing, symbolism, and close to home allure. Making a convincing story requires a comprehension of your crowd's social foundation, interests, and profound triggers. Whether conveying an attempt to sell something, an inspirational discourse, or an enticing contention, inserting your message inside a story structure upgrades its effect and memorability.

The capacity to understand people on a deeper level, the capacity to perceive and deal with feelings in oneself as well as other people, is a primary expertise for breathtaking influence. Feelings assume a focal part in direction, and a convincing communicator should be sensitive to the profound scene of their crowd. Compassion, genuineness, and profound reverberation fabricate an association that rises above judicious contentions.

While positive feelings can be utilized to make energy and purchase in, the affirmation and approval of pessimistic feelings are similarly significant. Tending to worries, easing fears, and showing veritable comprehension of the difficulties looked by your crowd cultivates trust and believability. The ability to understand anyone on a deeper level empowers you to explore the unpredictable territory of human feelings, changing likely snags into open doors for influence.

The influential ability stretches out past individual collaborations to envelop the domain of collective vibes and initiative. Pioneers, by definition, are forces to be reckoned with who guide and rouse others toward a typical vision or objective. Successful initiative requires an unmistakable vision and vital intuition as well as the capacity to energize support, fabricate agreement, and explore different viewpoints.

Initiative influence includes making a convincing story that lines up with the qualities and goals of the group. Imparting a common vision encourages a feeling of direction and solidarity, propelling people to contribute their earnest attempts. A convincing pioneer rouses trust, supports coordinated effort, and adjusts their correspondence style to resound with the different characters inside the group.

With regards to hierarchical authority, influence turns into a device for driving change and collecting support for key drives. Change the executives intrinsically includes defeating obstruction, and convincing correspondence is instrumental in tending to worries, encouraging an uplifting perspective, and imparting trust in the imagined change. A pioneer's capacity to explore opposition, convey really, and move aggregate responsibility is urgent in the progress of hierarchical change endeavors.

The specialty of influence isn't bound to the verbally expressed or composed word; it reaches out to the domain of visual correspondence. In an undeniably visual and computerized world, the effect of pictures, plan, and sight and sound couldn't possibly be more significant. Visual components have the ability to pass on complex data, summon feelings, and improve the memorability of a message.

Compelling visual influence includes the essential utilization of illustrations, pictures, and plan standards to supplement and support verbal messages. Whether in introductions, showcasing materials, or online substance, visual components ought to line up with the general story and appeal to the stylish inclinations of the interest group. The cooperative energy among visual and verbal correspondence improves the generally convincing effect and works with better maintenance of data.

In the advanced age, the stages and channels for correspondence have extended dramatically. Online entertainment, specifically, has arisen as a powerful field for influence, backing, and impact. The capacity to explore the elements of online entertainment requires a comprehension of the exceptional qualities of every stage, the inclinations of assorted crowds, and the force of viral substance.

Web-based entertainment influence includes making convincing messages as well as drawing in with the crowd in a dynamic and genuine way. Building a web-based entertainment presence that reverberates with your interest group requires consistency, responsiveness, and the essential utilization of visual and composed content. The viral idea of virtual entertainment enhances the span and effect of convincing messages, making it an important instrument for people and associations the same.

In any case, the universality of virtual entertainment additionally presents difficulties, as deception, polarization, and algorithmic predispositions can impact the spread of messages. Moral contemplations should direct the utilization of virtual entertainment for influence, with a promise to precision, straightforwardness, and capable commitment. Online entertainment's true capacity as a power for positive change lies in the possession of the people who employ it with honesty and a real longing to add to significant discussions.

In the domain of exchange, influence takes on an essential aspect. Discussion is innately a course of compromise, requiring the capacity to impact the viewpoints and choices of the gatherings in question. Powerful exchange influence includes figuring out the interests, inspirations, and needs of the two sides, making mutual benefit arrangements, and building a cooperative air.

Key components of enticing exchange incorporate readiness, undivided attention, and the capacity to approach proposition in a way that tends to the requirements, everything being equal. Mediators should be adroit at building affinity, overseeing clashes, and adjusting their methodology in light of the advancing elements of the discussion cycle. The craft of give and take and settling on something worth agreeing on is key to effective exchange influence.

In the lawful domain, influence is a fundamental part of backing. Attorneys, in communicating their perspectives, should utilize enticing strategies to persuade judges, juries, and contradicting counsel. Lawful influence includes not just the dominance of legitimate contentions and proof yet in addition the capacity to develop a convincing story that lines up with the standards of equity.

The specialty of influence in regulation reaches out to composed reports, oral contentions, and the assessment of witnesses. Lawful experts should be talented in introducing complex legitimate ideas in a way that is open and powerful to different crowds. The moral obligations of legitimate influence incorporate trustworthiness, regard for fair treatment, and a pledge to the quest for equity instead of simple triumph.

In the domain of promoting and publicizing, influence is the soul of accomplishment. Brands try to convince buyers to pick their items or administrations over other options, and compelling promoting influence includes figuring out customer conduct, making an extraordinary incentive, and building a brand story that reverberates.

The brain research of shopper navigation is a mind boggling exchange of level-headed and profound variables. Showcasing influence use the standards of marking, narrating, and close to home enticement for make an association with the main interest group. The essential utilization of language, visuals, and promoting channels improves the enticing effect and impacts shopper insights.

Moral contemplations in promoting influence incorporate straightforwardness, honesty, and a pledge to following through on guaranteed esteem. Tricky practices might yield transient gains however dissolve trust and harm brand notoriety over the long haul. Genuineness, client centricity, and capable promoting add to supportable outcome in the serious scene.

In the political field, influence is a foundation of discretionary missions and administration. Political pioneers should convince citizens to help their appointment, parties should convince the electorate to line up with their belief systems, and policymakers should convince the general population to embrace their drives. Political influence includes the craft of outlining issues, building alliances, and exploring the intricacies of general assessment.

The job of political influence stretches out past constituent cycles to the domain of administration. Chosen authorities should constantly draw in with the general population, convey strategy choices, and fabricate agreement on regulative issues. Straightforwardness, responsibility, and responsiveness are fundamental parts of moral political influence, guaranteeing that pioneers stay associated with the necessities and desires of the electorate.

In the scholastic circle, the craft of influence is fundamental to the fields of educating, exploration, and scholarly talk. Teachers should convince understudies to draw in with course material, specialists should convince friends of the legitimacy of their discoveries, and researchers should convince perusers of the meaning of their commitments. Influence in scholarly community includes the authority of manner of speaking, proof based argumentation, and the capacity to convey complex ideas with lucidity.

In logical exploration, influence is entwined with the course of friend audit and distribution. Analysts should convince diary editors and commentators of the thoroughness, legitimacy, and oddity of their work. Established researchers, thusly, takes part in an aggregate course of influence, with proof and contemplated argumentation filling in as the money of scholarly talk.

The interdisciplinary idea of contemporary difficulties requires a union of information and joint effort across different fields. Influence turns into a device for connecting disciplinary holes, encouraging interdisciplinary exchange, and collecting support for cooperative drives. Viable interdisciplinary influence includes the capacity to impart across specific spaces, decipher complex ideas for different crowds, and fabricate a mutual perspective of perplexing issues.

The moral components of influence in scholarly community envelop scholarly trustworthiness, regard for different viewpoints, and a promise to the quest for information to improve society. In a period of data overflow, the obligation of researchers to take part in moral influence is vital to keeping up with the respectability and believability of scholarly talk.

3.1 The principles of persuasion and their application in communication

The standards of influence, well established in the domains of brain research and correspondence, have been a subject of interest and study for a really long time. From old rationalists to current researchers, the mission to comprehend how people can impact and persuade others has been a determined undertaking. In this investigation, we dig into the center standards of influence and their nuanced applications in the mind boggling scene of correspondence.

At the core of powerful correspondence lies the correspondence standard, an idea grounded in the human tendency to bring favors back. Dr. Robert Cialdini, a prestigious social clinician, clarifies this guideline in his fundamental work, "Impact: The Brain research of Influence." Correspondence recommends that people feel a sense of urgency to answer in kind when somebody has worked on something for them. This natural craving for decency and equilibrium turns into an incredible asset in the possession of persuaders.

Consider a situation where a companion loans some assistance in a period of scarcity. The beneficiary of this blessing, deliberately or not, encounters a feeling of obligation. This mental obligation lays the preparation for the persuader to make a solicitation or present a thought, profiting by the correspondence rule. Whether in private connections or expert settings, understanding and utilizing correspondence can fundamentally upgrade one's abilities to entice.

One more essential rule of influence is shortage, featuring the human inclination to want what is seen as intriguing or hard to get. This guideline takes advantage of the apprehension about passing up a great opportunity (FOMO) and highlights the effect of restricted accessibility on navigation. Shortage makes a need to get a move on, inciting people to act quickly to get an important open door or asset.

In showcasing, the shortage guideline is frequently utilized to drive purchaser conduct. Restricted time offers, selective deliveries, and item deficiencies generally trigger a need to get a move on, convincing people to settle on buying choices speedily. By decisively integrating shortage into correspondence, persuaders can invigorate activity and guide their crowd toward an ideal result.

The guideline of power highlights the impact employed by believable and learned figures. Individuals are normally disposed to trust and follow those apparent as specialists in a specific space. Whether it's a doctor recommending a treatment plan or an idea chief sharing experiences, the power guideline highlights the enticing effect of mastery.

In the domain of correspondence, securing oneself as an authority includes displaying applicable information, experience, and certifications. This could be accomplished using information, insights, or supports from trustworthy sources. In any case, it's essential to keep up with validness and straightforwardness, as believability can be effortlessly disintegrated on the off chance that people see a crisscross between guaranteed mastery and real information.

Consistency, as a guideline of influence, investigates the human propensity to line up with past responsibilities and decisions. When an individual focuses on a specific position or activity, there is a mental drive to keep up with consistency in resulting conduct. This guideline is profoundly interwoven with the requirement for mental self view upkeep and the uneasiness related with mental cacophony.

With regards to correspondence, persuaders can use the consistency guideline by getting little responsibilities prior to introducing bigger solicitations. By getting starting purchase in or understanding, people are bound to maintain a steady position in resulting cooperations. This approach limits opposition and lines up with the intrinsic human tendency to keep up with agreement inside one's conviction framework.

Social confirmation, an idea underlining the effect of friend impact, is a strong power in the domain of influence. At the point when people are dubious about a choice, they frequently focus on the activities and decisions of others for direction. This dependence on expressive gestures is profoundly imbued in human way of behaving and is a vital driver of similarity.

In the time of web-based entertainment, social evidence has acquired extraordinary unmistakable quality. Client surveys, tributes, and supports act as computerized indications of social confirmation, forming discernments and affecting choices. From picking a café in light of online surveys to choosing an item embraced by a web-based entertainment powerhouse, the standard of social confirmation penetrates different parts of contemporary correspondence.

Understanding the standards of influence is just the initial step; their viable application requires a nuanced approach that thinks about the unique circumstance, crowd, and explicit objectives of correspondence. In relational correspondence, the specialty of influence frequently includes undivided attention and compassionate comprehension. By adjusting oneself to the requirements, concerns, and points of view of others, persuaders can tailor their messages to resound with the qualities and needs of their crowd.

Sympathy, a foundation of successful correspondence, includes the capacity to comprehend and discuss the thoughts of another. At the point when people feel appreciated and comprehended, they are bound to be available to influence. Compassionate correspondence cultivates a feeling of association and compatibility, establishing a helpful climate for the trading of thoughts and viewpoints.

Past sympathy, viable influence requires a sharp familiarity with social subtleties and variety. In a globalized world, where correspondence traverses different social scenes, a one-size-fits-all approach is frequently lacking. Aversion to social contrasts, phonetic varieties, and accepted practices is fundamental for making messages that reverberate across different crowds.

The force of narrating in influence couldn't possibly be more significant. People are innately attracted to stories that inspire feeling and significance. Whether in private stories, contextual analyses, or figurative stories, narrating adds a convincing aspect to correspondence. By outlining messages as stories, persuaders connect with the objective psyche as well as the profound center of their crowd.

In the computerized age, the medium through which correspondence happens assumes a crucial part in molding convincing methodologies. The ascent of web-based entertainment, web recordings, video content, and other computerized stages has changed the scene of correspondence. Every medium conveys its own remarkable properties and elements, requiring versatility in enticing methodologies.

Visual correspondence, specifically, has turned into a predominant power in the period of data over-burden. Infographics, recordings, and pictures can pass on complex messages more briefly and significantly than message alone. Persuaders who outfit the visual part of correspondence stand to catch consideration, improve maintenance, and inspire close to home reactions.

In the midst of the bunch devices and methods of influence, moral contemplations should stay foremost. The moral component of influence spins around straightforwardness, genuineness, and regard for the independence of people. Manipulative strategies that exploit weaknesses or bamboozle the crowd disintegrate trust as well as have the potential for long haul adverse results.

The morals of influence are particularly important in fields like promoting, where the line among influence and control can become obscured. Promoters should explore the fragile harmony between catching consideration and passing on precise data. The Government Exchange Commission (FTC) and other administrative bodies assume a significant part in setting rules and principles to guarantee moral practices in promoting and showcasing.

In political correspondence, a lot is on the line, and the moral aspect turns out to be much more articulated. The obligation to give honest data, stay away from deception, and regard the vote based process highlights the moral basic for political communicators. The ascent of falsehood in the advanced age further enhances the requirement for moral watchfulness in the domain of political influence.

The crossing point of influence and initiative is a powerful space where compelling correspondence is principal. Pioneers, whether in corporate settings, political fields, or local area associations, should become the best at influence to assemble support, move activity, and cultivate cooperation. The standards of influence become devices in the possession of pioneers, forming authoritative culture and impacting the course of aggregate undertakings.

Versatile administration, an idea promoted by Ronald Heifetz and Marty Linsky, underlines the capacity to explore change and prepare others despite complex difficulties. Influence is a focal part of versatile initiative, as pioneers should convey a convincing vision, impart certainty, and guide people through groundbreaking cycles. The standards of influence, when employed prudently, improve a pioneer's capacity to fabricate agreement and drive positive change.

Exchange, an expertise necessary to different parts of expert and individual life, depends vigorously on the standards of influence. Whether in business bargains, political undertakings, or relational contentions, mediators try to impact results in support of themselves. The craft of discussion includes a sensitive dance of decisiveness, sympathy, and key correspondence.

In the business domain, the standards of influence track down applications in advertising, deals, and client relations. Successful salesmen comprehend the mental triggers that instant people to pursue buying choices. From laying out compatibility to outlining item helps in a convincing way, deals experts influence to effectively explore the purchaser's excursion.

Client relations, an undeniably imperative part of business achievement, is complicatedly connected to convincing correspondence. Brands that focus on client experience perceive the significance of conveying quality items or administrations as well as developing positive connections. Influence in client relations includes undivided attention, responsiveness, and a pledge to addressing the requirements and assumptions for clients.

The standards of influence are similarly pertinent in the domain of advertising (PR), where molding general assessment and it are central to oversee notoriety. PR experts should explore the sensitive harmony among straightforwardness and vital correspondence. In the midst of emergency, the capacity to convey a story that reverberates with people in general turns into a basic part of emergency the executives.

The job of influence in lawful correspondence is multi-layered, reaching out from the court to public talk. Attorneys, as backers, influence powerful procedures to introduce unquestionable cases and influence the assessments of judges and juries. The specialty of way of talking, profoundly imbued in legitimate practices, stresses the enticing force of language and argumentation.

Past the court, lawful experts participate in open correspondence to shape popular assessment, impact strategy, and promoter for legitimate changes. The standards of influence are obvious in the creating of lawful contentions, the outlining of regulative recommendations, and the correspondence of complicated legitimate ideas to a more extensive crowd. Lawful communicators should explore the crossing point of influence and moral obligation, guaranteeing that their messages line up with the standards of equity and decency.

In the domain of medical services, viable correspondence is vital to patient consideration, general wellbeing drives, and clinical promotion. Medical services experts, from doctors to general wellbeing authorities, should utilize influence to support sound ways of behaving, pass on clinical data, and fabricate entrust with patients.

The specialist patient relationship, frequently viewed as a worldview of powerful correspondence, depends on the standards of influence to cultivate consistence with treatment designs and advance preventive consideration. Bedside way, an idea established in compassion and powerful correspondence, highlights the significance of establishing a positive and confiding in climate for patients.

General wellbeing efforts, resolving issues going from immunization attention to smoking suspension, influence influential correspondence techniques to impact conduct change on a cultural level. The progress of such missions depends on figuring out the assorted elements that impact individual and aggregate wellbeing choices.

The standards of influence reach out to the domains of schooling and the scholarly world, where compelling correspondence is fundamental to the growing experience. Educators, as communicators and facilitators of information, should connect with understudies, flash interest, and convey complex ideas in an engaging way. The specialty of educating includes a powerful exchange of influence, inspiration, and information move.

In scholastic exploration and distributing, the capacity to convince is obvious in the creating of examination recommendations, academic articles, and award applications. Analysts should successfully convey the meaning of their work, legitimize systemic decisions, and persuade peers regarding the legitimacy and importance of their discoveries. The friend survey process itself mirrors the utilization of influence inside the scholarly local area.

The advanced period has changed the scene of schooling, with internet learning stages, virtual study halls, and media assets becoming vital to the instructive experience. The standards of influence track down new roads of articulation in the plan of online courses, instructive substance, and intelligent opportunities for growth.

In the domain of relational connections, the standards of influence are ever-present, molding associations in relational intricacies, companionships, and heartfelt organizations. Compelling correspondence inside connections includes a fragile equilibrium of self-assuredness, undivided attention, and compassion. The capacity to communicate needs, arrange contrasts, and resolve clashes draws on the standards of influence.

Close connections, specifically, are fields where the standards of influence can significantly affect the elements between accomplices. From the underlying phases of romance to the drawn out upkeep of a relationship, people utilize convincing procedures to communicate love, resolve conflicts, and explore the intricacies of close to home closeness.

In familial connections, successful correspondence is fundamental for cultivating understanding and amicability. Guardians, in their job as parental figures and guides, influence to grant values, impart discipline, and support the close to home prosperity of their youngsters. Kin connections, as well, include discussion, split the difference, and the use of powerful procedures to explore the common spaces of day to day life.

In the more extensive cultural setting, the standards of influence are clear in developments for social change, activism, and promotion. Social developments, whether zeroed in on social liberties, ecological equity, or orientation fairness, depend on powerful correspondence to prepare support, bring issues to light, and impact fundamental change.

The elements of convincing correspondence in friendly developments include outlining accounts that resound with assorted crowds, utilizing social evidence to show boundless help, and countering contradicting perspectives. Grassroots activism, filled by enthusiastic people focused on a reason, frequently depends on the standards of influence to collect open consideration and impact strategy results.

In the political field, the standards of influence are used with specific strength. Political missions, discussions, and strategy promotion include the essential utilization of influential procedures to influence general assessment and secure electing support. Political pioneers, as expert communicators, should explore the intricacies of different electorates, media investigation, and advancing public opinion.

The approach of computerized correspondence stages has altered political talk, giving new channels to influence and commitment. Web-based entertainment, specifically, has turned into a landmark for contending stories, political informing, and the molding of public discernment. The standards of influence track down articulation in the making of viral substance, the development of online networks, and the essential utilization of information examination for designated informing.

The moral components of political influence come to the very front, with contemplations of honesty, straightforwardness, and regard for majority rule standards. The ascent of falsehood and the control of general assessment through computerized implies highlight the significance of moral cautiousness in political correspondence.

As we explore the complicated embroidery of enticing correspondence, it becomes apparent that the standards of influence are not disengaged ideas but rather interconnected strings woven into the texture of human connection. From the complexities of individual connections to the fabulous phases of political theater, the specialty of influence shapes the stories that characterize our common reality.

3.2 Building credibility and trust with your audience

Building believability and entrust with a crowd of people is a multi-layered try that lies at the core of powerful correspondence. Whether in proficient settings, relational connections, or public talk, believability and trust are irreplaceable components that support effective communications. In this investigation, we dig into the critical elements and techniques engaged with developing validity and trust, perceiving that these characteristics are central to cultivating significant associations and accomplishing positive results.

Genuineness as the Foundation

At the center of building believability and trust is realness. Realness includes adjusting one's words and activities to certified convictions and values. It is the establishment whereupon validity is built. At the point when people sense genuineness in a communicator, they are bound to see that individual as dependable. Legitimacy makes an association by flagging straightforwardness and genuineness, laying the basis for the foundation of trust.

In the domain of authority, genuineness is a central trait that recognizes viable pioneers from the people who battle to collect trust. Pioneers who legitimately express their qualities, recognize their weaknesses, and show consistency among words and deeds motivate trust in their adherents. This realness resounds in snapshots of achievement as well as in the midst of challenge or difficulty, supporting the pioneer's believability.

Ability and Skill

Validity is innately connected to capability and aptitude. People are bound to believe the people who exhibit an elevated degree of information and capability in their separate spaces. Skill can be displayed through capabilities, experience, and a history of fruitful achievements. Whether in an expert setting or as a power figure in a particular field, the impression of capability contributes fundamentally to the structure of believability.

In the business world, for instance, clients are more disposed to entrust organizations that are driven by people with a demonstrated history and a profound comprehension of their industry. A similar rule applies to experts trying to secure themselves as specialists in their fields. By consistently growing their insight, keeping up to date with industry patterns, and displaying their mastery, people can improve their believability and, thus, encourage trust.

Dependability and Consistency

Unwavering quality and consistency structure the bedrock of trust. People who reliably follow through on their commitments and commitments are seen as solid, making a feeling of steadfastness that fortifies trust over the long haul. This unwavering quality reaches out past gathering cutoff times or satisfying responsibilities; it envelops the consistency of conduct, correspondence, and navigation.

In relational connections, unwavering quality is much of the time exhibited through being reliable in the two words and activities. At the point when somebody reliably finishes responsibilities, imparts straightforwardly, and acts typically, trust normally creates. A similar guideline applies in hierarchical settings, where pioneers who display consistency in navigation and correspondence cultivate a culture of trust among their colleagues.

Compelling Correspondence and Straightforwardness

Correspondence is a useful asset in the stockpile of validity building. Clear, legit, and straightforward correspondence lays out an open and bona fide exchange, adding to the impression of dependability. Compelling communicators pass on their messages with clearness, effectively pay attention to other people, and explore complex subjects with straightforwardness.

With regards to authority, straightforward correspondence is particularly essential. Pioneers who share data transparently, address concerns proactively, and impart the reasoning behind choices encourage a climate of trust inside their groups. Straightforwardness mitigates vulnerability and assists people with feeling educated and included, building up the believability of pioneers.

The ability to understand anyone at their core and Compassion

The capacity to understand people on a deeper level, enveloping mindfulness, social mindfulness, self-guideline, and relationship the executives, assumes a critical part in building validity and trust. People with high capacity to understand anyone on a profound level are receptive to their own feelings and those of others, empowering them to explore relational elements with responsiveness and compassion.

Compassion, specifically, is a strong power in laying out trust. At the point when people feel comprehended, approved, and really focused on, trust normally thrives. Sympathetic communicators listen effectively, try to figure out the points of view of others, and show a certifiable worry for the prosperity of those they connect with. In initiative, compassion is a key part for making a positive hierarchical culture based on common trust and regard.

Honesty and Moral Direct

Honesty is a non-debatable part of believability and trust. It includes sticking to a bunch of moral standards, keeping up with consistency among values and activities, and maintaining a feeling of trustworthiness and reasonableness. People who work with uprightness are seen as principled and dependable, gaining the appreciation and certainty of everyone around them.

In the corporate world, moral lead is a foundation of hierarchical believability. Organizations that focus on honesty in their strategic approaches, treat workers and clients decently, and maintain moral guidelines are bound to assemble getting through entrust with partners. The disintegration of trust because of moral breaches can have significant and enduring outcomes, highlighting the vital significance of respectability in believability building.

Receptiveness to Criticism and Learning

The capacity to get criticism with lowliness and a guarantee to persistent learning contributes fundamentally to validity. People who are available to productive analysis, recognize their areas of progress, and effectively look for open doors for development are seen as congenial and credible. This transparency cultivates a climate of trust, as it shows an eagerness to develop and adjust.

Pioneers who energize a culture of criticism inside their groups make a mentally place of refuge for coordinated effort and development. At the point when colleagues feel happy with giving criticism and see pioneers effectively answering it, trust thrives. This dynamic mirrors a promise to shared development and improvement, reinforcing the texture of trust inside the hierarchical setting.

Building Validity in the Computerized Age

In a time overwhelmed by advanced correspondence, the techniques for building believability and trust have developed. Online presence, virtual entertainment commitment, and computerized standing assume significant parts in forming discernments. Dealing with one's computerized impression with care and deliberateness is fundamental for building and keeping up with believability in the advanced domain.

Steady and legitimate marking across advanced stages adds to the foundation of validity. Whether through proficient profiles, web-based entertainment posts, or online commitments, people can shape their computerized personalities in manners that line up with their qualities and skill. Insightful curation of online substance permits people to feature their capability and credibility to a worldwide crowd.

Commitment to online networks, thought authority, and the sharing of important experiences add to the foundation of advanced validity. By partaking in significant conversations, adding to industry discussions, and giving significant substance, people can situate themselves as believable voices inside their web-based networks.

Be that as it may, the computerized scene additionally presents difficulties, as deception, online assaults, and the fast spread of bits of gossip can compromise one's advanced validity. Cautiousness in overseeing on the web notoriety, tending to deception proactively, and building a strong internet based presence are pivotal parts of believability working in the computerized age.

Revamping Trust After Breakdowns

Definitely, trust might be tried and, on occasion, broken. Whether because of correspondence slips, moral infringement, or unanticipated conditions, the most common way of remaking trust is a sensitive however feasible undertaking.

Recognizing Errors: When trust is compromised, recognizing botches straightforwardly is a basic initial step. Whether an individual or an association, getting a sense of ownership with mistakes shows trustworthiness and a pledge to responsibility.

Correspondence and Straightforwardness: Open correspondence about the breakdown of trust and straightforwardly sharing designs for development are fundamental parts of the revamping system. Tending to worries, responding to questions, and giving a guide to restorative activities add to reconstructing believability.

Steady and Solid Way of behaving: Modifying trust requires predictable and dependable conduct over the long haul. People should exhibit through their activities that the variables adding to the breakdown have been tended to, and a pledge to reliable lead has been reaffirmed.

Tuning in and Answering: Effectively paying attention to the worries and criticism of those impacted by the breakdown is pivotal. Answering with compassion and a veritable craving to comprehend the viewpoints of others shows a promise to remaking trust.

Setting Reasonable Assumptions: Laying out sensible assumptions for the reconstructing system is significant. Trust, once broken, carves out opportunity to revamp. Setting straightforward courses of events and achievements for progress oversees assumptions and exhibits a genuine obligation to the interaction.

3.3 Utilizing rhetorical devices to enhance persuasive communication

The craft of influence has been a basic part of human correspondence for quite a long time, and over the entire course of time, explanatory gadgets have filled in as integral assets to improve the viability of powerful messages. Expository gadgets incorporate a different cluster of etymological procedures and complex techniques that are intended to connect with, convince, and enrapture a group of people. In this investigation, we dive into the universe of logical gadgets, looking at how they can be decisively utilized to raise powerful correspondence across different settings.

Grasping Expository Gadgets

Expository gadgets are phonetic devices used to improve the outflow of thoughts and inspire explicit reactions from a group of people. These gadgets work at the degrees of language, design, and generally speaking sythesis, impacting how messages are seen and recalled. They are utilized in proper addresses as well as in ordinary discussions, composed talk, publicizing, and different types of media.

One central expository gadget is the utilization of similarities and analogies. Relationships draw matches between two unmistakable ideas to feature likenesses and enlighten complex thoughts. Similitudes, then again, include depicting one thing as far as another, making clear and inventive associations. By utilizing relationships and allegories, communicators can improve on complex ideas, make conceptual thoughts more unmistakable, and appeal to the feelings of their crowd.

The Force of Redundancy

Redundancy is an expository gadget that includes the conscious reuse of words, expressions, or designs to build up central issues and improve memorability. Reiteration can take different structures, like the redundancy of sounds (similar sounding word usage), the reiteration of words toward the start of progressive provisos (anaphora), or the reiteration of words toward the finish of progressive statements (epistrophe).

Martin Luther Lord Jr's. famous "I Have a Fantasy" discourse is a demonstration of the powerful effect of redundancy. The purposeful utilization of anaphora, with phrases like "I have a fantasy," not just underlined the speaker's vision for a superior future yet in addition made a musical and vital rhythm that resounded with the crowd. Redundancy can impart a feeling of accentuation, desperation, and solidarity, making it a strong gadget in enticing correspondence.

The utilization of feelings, known as tenderness, is a focal part of influential correspondence. Explanatory gadgets that enticement for feelings can bring out compassion, compassion, or enthusiasm, encouraging a more profound association with the crowd. Methods like accounts, individual stories, and close to home language are regularly utilized to get profound reactions.

Think about the effect of an individual story in a powerful setting. Sharing an interesting story makes a profound extension between the communicator and the crowd. The crowd is bound to be moved and impacted when they can interface genuinely with the message. By taking advantage of the profound part of human experience, communicators can fortify their enticing allure and have an enduring effect.

The Craft of Logos: Utilizing Rationale and Thinking

Logos, the enticement for rationale and thinking, is one more vital component of convincing correspondence. Explanatory gadgets that improve the consistent allure of a message incorporate similarities, insights, and arguments. Relationships, as referenced prior, draw matches between various ideas, assisting with explaining complex thoughts by contrasting them with additional natural ones. Insights give observational proof, supporting the genuine premise of a contention. Arguments include a consistent design wherein two premises lead to a decision, adding a layer of rational thinking to the correspondence.

In a business show, for instance, a speaker could utilize measurements to help the viability of a proposed methodology. By introducing information and mathematical proof, the speaker improves the intelligent allure of the message, making it more persuading for a group of people that values experimental help. The essential utilization of logos adds to the general enticement of the correspondence.

Catching Consideration with Similar sounding word usage and Sound similarity

The sonic nature of language assumes a huge part in catching the consideration of a group of people. Similar sounding word usage, the redundancy of beginning consonant sounds in closeness, and sound similarity, the reiteration of vowel sounds, add a cadenced and melodic aspect to language. These gadgets make the correspondence more captivating as well as add to the memorability of the message.

Think about the renowned line from Shakespeare's Hamlet: "To be, or not to be, that is the issue." The similar sounding word usage of the "b" and "t" sounds makes a musical quality that improves the effect of Hamlet's consideration. Likewise, the conscious utilization of sound similarity can make an agreeable and melodic quality in language, adding to its stylish allure.

Underlying Gadgets: Parallelism and Direct opposite

Primary gadgets, like parallelism and direct opposite, add to the general lucidness and effect of convincing correspondence. Parallelism includes utilizing a predictable syntactic design across expressions or sentences, making a feeling of equilibrium and evenness. This strategy upgrades lucidity and stresses central issues.

For example, in John F. Kennedy's debut address, he broadly declared, "Thus, my kindred Americans: ask not how your nation can help you — ask how you can help your country." The equal construction of the sentences adds a cadenced quality as well as builds up the call to urban obligation.

Absolute opposite, then again, includes comparing differentiating thoughts inside similar sentence or adjoining sentences. This makes a feeling of resistance, underlining the qualification among ideas and causing to notice the inborn strain. Direct opposite can be a strong gadget for featuring differentiations and making central issues more essential.

The Craft of Influential Game plan: Peak and Disappointment

The game plan of thoughts inside a correspondence is a vital part of influence. Two logical gadgets that assume a part in organizing the power of a message are peak and disappointment. Peak includes organizing thoughts in rising request of significance or power, working toward a pinnacle. This slow expansion in force makes a feeling of expectation and underscores the meaning of the last point.

Let-down, then again, includes organizing thoughts in plummeting request of significance or power. This construction can be utilized for comedic impact or to make shock. The surprising movement from more serious to less extraordinary focuses can catch the crowd's consideration and have an enduring effect.

Making Distinctive Symbolism with Metaphors and Poetic overstatement

Distinctive symbolism has the ability to inspire solid mental pictures, making messages more noteworthy and effective. Expository gadgets, for example, metaphors and poetic exaggeration are instrumental in making striking and creative language. A comparison includes looking at two dissimilar to things utilizing "like" or "as," while poetic overstatement includes embellishment for accentuation.

Think about the effect of a very much created likeness: "The night sky was basically as dim as coal." This examination quickly invokes a striking mental picture, upgrading the spellbinding nature of the correspondence. Poetic exaggeration, when utilized wisely, can add accentuation and make a vital impression. For instance, "I've let you know multiple times to tidy up your room" utilizes poetic exaggeration to stress the recurrence of the solicitation.

Vital Utilization of Implication and Style

The selection of words, known as style, assumes a vital part in molding the tone and effect of enticing correspondence. The undertone of words — close to home or social affiliations that go past their exacting implications — adds layers of significance to the message. Good implications can bring out positive feelings, while pessimistic undertones can impact discernments somewhere new.

Think about the contrast between saying "frugal" and "modest." While the two words might allude to thriftiness, "frugal" conveys an encouraging implication, proposing savvy and reasonable monetary propensities, though "modest" may convey a regrettable underlying meaning, suggesting an absence of value or miserliness.

Fitting Expository Gadgets to Crowd and Setting

A fundamental part of successful influential correspondence is the capacity to fit logical gadgets to the particular crowd and setting. Various crowds answer explanatory systems in changed ways, and communicators should be sensitive to the inclinations, values, and assumptions for their interest group.

In political talk, for instance, a speaker may decisively utilize logical gadgets that resound with the qualities and worries of a specific segment. Utilizing language and complex components that line up with the social and etymological subtleties of the crowd improves the influential effect of the message.

Moral Contemplations in Enticing Correspondence

While explanatory gadgets can essentially improve the viability of enticing correspondence, moral contemplations should stay vital. The essential utilization of language and elaborate components shouldn't stray into control or trickery. Communicators have an obligation to maintain the standards of genuineness, straightforwardness, and regard for the independence of the crowd.

In promoting, for example, the utilization of poetic overstatement to underline item includes is normal. Notwithstanding, going too far into bogus or deceiving claims disregards moral principles. The moral utilization of logical gadgets includes a promise to honesty, staying away from the control of feelings for unscrupulous purposes.

3.4 Persuasive speeches and writings

Influence, as a key part of human correspondence, tracks down articulation in different structures, with convincing discourses and compositions standing apart as strong vehicles for passing on messages, impacting feelings, and motivating activity. Whether conveyed from a platform, composed on a page, or shared through computerized stages, powerful correspondence looks to influence the considerations and ways of behaving of a group of people. In this investigation, we dig into the subtleties of convincing addresses and works, analyzing the key components, procedures, and moral contemplations that shape these compelling types of articulation.

Grasping Influence: An Intricate Interchange of Variables

At its center, influence includes the purposeful work to impact the convictions, mentalities, or ways of behaving of others. It works on the reason that correspondence isn't just a trade of data yet a powerful cycle that can get a reaction. Influence draws on a different arrangement of instruments, including expository gadgets, close to home requests, and coherent thinking, to create messages that reverberate with the crowd.

Enticing discourses and works, while sharing the all-encompassing objective of affecting, manifest in particular ways, each customized to the attributes and inclinations of the medium. In an enticing discourse, the expressed word becomes the overwhelming focus, depending on the speaker's conveyance, tone, and presence to connect with the crowd. Then again, enticing composing tackles the composed word, taking into account cautious thought, update, and the essential utilization of language and construction.

The Force of Powerful Discourses: Rhetoric as an Artistic expression

By and large, enticing discourses play had a vital impact in forming general assessment, stirring developments, and mobilizing networks. The expressive custom, tracing all the way back to antiquated human advancements, praises the excellencies of gifted speakers who can dazzle, motivate, and move crowds through the power of their words. Striking figures like Winston Churchill, Martin Luther Ruler Jr., and Cicero embody the getting through effect of powerful discourses.

One sign of influential talks is the essential utilization of logical gadgets. These semantic apparatuses, going from similar sounding word usage and similitudes to redundancy and parallelism, improve the imaginativeness and convincingness of the expressed word. For example, Martin Luther Lord Jr's. "I Have a Fantasy" discourse unbelievably utilized redundancy and similitudes to convey a strong vision of racial uniformity, making a permanent imprint on the social liberties development.

Organizing Enticing Addresses: The Force of Plan

Viable plan is a foundation of enticing discourses. Aristotle's traditional model of influence, including ethos (validity), feeling (feeling), and logos (rationale), gives a system to sorting out enticing messages. The presentation catches consideration, lays out believability, and establishes the vibe for the discourse. The body creates central issues, utilizing proof, tales, and requests to feeling to reinforce the contention. The end supports the message, having an enduring impact on the crowd.

Inside this structure, the essential game plan of thoughts adds to the intelligence and effect of the discourse. Peak, the plan of thoughts in climbing request of significance or force, works toward a pinnacle, making a feeling of expectation. Let-down, where thoughts are organized in dropping request, can be utilized for comedic impact or to amaze the crowd. The smart course of action of thoughts upgrades the influence of the general message.

Conveyance and Nonverbal Correspondence

In powerful talks, the conveyance is all around as critical as the substance. Compelling speakers give fastidious consideration to their nonverbal correspondence, incorporating motions, looks, stance, and vocal tone. These components add to the speaker's moxy, validity, and capacity to interface with the crowd. A speaker who keeps in touch, utilizes expressive motions, and regulates their voice can convey certainty and genuineness, building up the powerful effect of the message.

Think about the enticing force of non-verbal communication in political speech. A competitor's stance, looks, and signals can shape impression of credibility and initiative. Similarly, a powerful orator's vivified conveyance can stimulate a group of people, improving the receptivity to the message. Nonverbal correspondence, when lined up with the substance, intensifies the influential allure of the discourse.

Tackling the Composed Word: Enticing Composing Techniques

Powerful composition, while without the prompt input of a live crowd, has its own arrangement of assets and difficulties. It considers careful making, modification, and the joining of many explanatory gadgets. Whether as papers, articles, or promoting duplicate, convincing composing tries to draw in perusers, fabricate a convincing case, and brief activity.

Creating Convincing Expositions: A Fragile Equilibrium of Logos, Ethos, and Feeling

Convincing papers are a typical type of composed influence, frequently experienced in scholar, proficient, or editorial settings. The design of a convincing paper commonly incorporates a presentation that presents the proposal, body sections that foster supporting contentions, and an end that builds up the primary concerns and calls for activity.

In the domain of enticing expositions, a fragile equilibrium of logos, ethos, and tenderness is fundamental. Logos includes introducing intelligent thinking, proof, and contentions that enticement for the judicious psyche of the peruser. Ethos focuses on laying out the validity and authority of the essayist, causing trust in the crowd. Feeling, like its part in talks, requests to the feelings of the peruser, cultivating an association and impacting perspectives.

Consider an exposition supporting for natural protection. The author might introduce logical information (logos) to highlight the criticalness of the issue, lay out their accreditations as a natural researcher (ethos), and consolidate stories or sincerely charged language to summon compassion for the planet (sentiment). This mix of enticing components upgrades the exposition's general effect.

Vital Utilization of Language: Word usage, Meaning, and Tone

In powerful composition, the selection of words, known as style, uses significant impact. Essayists decisively select words with explicit implications — profound or social affiliations — expecting to shape the peruser's insight. Encouraging implications can inspire good feelings, while pessimistic meanings can present a need to get a move on or concern.

The tone of convincing composing is another basic variable. Tone envelops the mentality and close to home position of the author toward the subject and crowd. An enticing exposition might utilize a tone that is decisive, sympathetic, or even comical, contingent upon the expository objectives and the idea of the crowd. Tone adds to the general ethos of the author, impacting how perusers see the message.

Interesting to the Peruser's Creative mind: Symbolism, Representations, and Similarities

Convincing composing frequently use the force of clear symbolism to draw in the peruser's creative mind. The utilization of allegories, similarities, and distinct language makes mental pictures that upgrade the peruser's comprehension and close to home association with the subject. Consider the effect of a similitude like "time is a cheat." This figurative articulation conveys time getting endlessly, adding a layer of close to home reverberation to the message.

Similarities, which draw matches between various ideas, can work on complex thoughts and make them more interesting. For example, clearing up a complex logical interaction by comparing it for a natural ordinary movement helps overcome any barrier between the new and the known, supporting perception and influence.

Making an Influential Account: Narrating as an Amazing asset

Narrating is an immortal and strong device in powerful correspondence. Whether in talks or compositions, stories can enrapture crowds, bring out compassion, and pass on messages in a critical way. Viable narrating includes creating a convincing story curve, presenting engaging characters or situations, and building strain and goal.

Consider an influential paper upholding for civil rights. The essayist might wind around a story that presents people impacted by foundational imbalance, giving a human face to the more extensive issue. By sharing individual stories, the essayist can evoke compassion, make a need to keep moving, and brief perusers to think about the cultural ramifications of the issue.

Interesting to Various Crowds: Fitting Enticing Messages

One of the signs of powerful influence is the capacity to fit messages to various crowds. Convincing correspondence isn't one-size-fits-all; it requires a comprehension of the different qualities, convictions, and inclinations of the main interest group. Journalists and speakers adroit at influence can adjust their language, tone, and requests to reverberate with explicit gatherings.

In showcasing, for instance, enticing messages should be made with a profound comprehension of the objective customer segment. The language used to advance an extravagance item might vary essentially from that utilized for a regular ware.

Effective sponsors are sensitive to the qualities and desires of their interest group, fitting influential messages to line up with these variables.

The Moral Goal: Genuineness, Straightforwardness, and Regard

While influence is an incredible asset, it accompanies moral obligations. Scholars and speakers have an obligation to maintain standards of trustworthiness, straightforwardness, and regard for their crowd. Moral influence includes introducing data honestly, keeping away from control, and regarding the independence of people to go with informed choices.

Chapter 4

The Impact of Language and Tone

Language and tone are useful assets that shape our correspondence and impact how we are seen by others. Whether spoken or composed, the words we pick and the manner in which we convey them can significantly affect our connections, our work, and our general outcome in different parts of life.

One of the vital parts of language is its capacity to convey meaning. The words we use convey explicit implications, and the manner in which we string them together structures sentences that offer our viewpoints and thoughts. Nonetheless, it's not just about passing on data; language likewise assumes a vital part in forming our feelings and impacting the feelings of those we speak with. The tone, or the profound nature of our language, adds one more layer to our correspondence, influencing how our words are gotten.

In proficient settings, the effect of language and tone is especially huge. Whether in the work environment or during business cooperations, compelling correspondence is fundamental for building solid connections and making progress. The selection of words and the tone wherein they are conveyed can decide the degree of trust and coordinated effort in a group, impact dynamic cycles, and even influence the generally speaking corporate culture.

In the work environment, lucidity and accuracy are fundamental. Vagueness in correspondence can prompt mistaken assumptions, disarray, and expected clashes. In this way, the decision of language becomes pivotal in passing on messages precisely and productively. Clear and succinct language helps in articulating thoughts and assumptions, diminishing the probability of misinterpretations.

Also, the tone utilized in proficient correspondence sets the climate for cooperation. A positive and deferential tone cultivates a sound workplace, advancing collaboration and inventiveness. On the other hand, a negative or ill bred tone can make strain, disintegrate trust, and frustrate efficiency. Pioneers who excel at offsetting decisiveness with compassion will more often than not make a good work culture where representatives feel esteemed and spurred.

Past the working environment, language and tone assume an essential part in private connections. Viable correspondence is the foundation of solid connections, whether they are familial, heartfelt, or companionships. The words we pick can either reinforce the bonds we share with others or make distance and strain.

In heartfelt connections, for instance, the effect of language and tone is clear in the manner couples speak with one another. Communicating affection and appreciation in an uplifting vibe can upgrade closeness and fortify the profound association. Then again, cruel or basic language can prompt hatred and profound distance. Couples who are aware of their language and tone will generally explore clashes all the more actually and support satisfying connections.

Additionally, in relational peculiarities, the selection of words can shape the general environment inside the family. Guardians who utilize empowering language and an uplifting vibe add to the close to home prosperity of their youngsters. On the other hand, consistent analysis or negative language can meaningfully affect a youngster's confidence and emotional wellness. Successful correspondence inside families isn't just about the trading of data yet in addition about establishing a sustaining and steady climate.

In companionships, the effect of language and tone is obvious in the manner companions impart and connect with one another. Steady language and an uplifting vibe encourage trust and develop the obligations of fellowship. Running against the norm, on the off chance that companions reliably utilize terrible words or embrace a negative tone, it can strain the relationship and lead to errors.

In the computerized age, where a lot of our correspondence happens through composed text, the effect of language and tone is enhanced. Virtual entertainment stages, messages, and informing applications have become essential method for communication, and the words we pick in these computerized spaces can have broad outcomes.

Via online entertainment, for example, the tone of our posts and remarks can shape how others see us. Positive and valuable language adds to a sound internet based local area, while negative or fierce language can prompt web-based clashes and stressed connections. The shortfall of non-verbal prompts in computerized correspondence goes with the decision of words considerably more basic, as there is no manner of speaking or non-verbal communication to give setting.

Email correspondence in proficient settings is another field where language and tone assume a critical part. Misjudged tones in messages can prompt pointless struggles and strain among partners. In this way, people should be aware of the language they use and the tone they pass in composed correspondence on to guarantee clearness and stay away from errors.

Also, the effect of language and tone reaches out to public talk and cultural cooperations. In the domain of governmental issues and public undertakings, the words utilized by pioneers can shape general assessment and impact the course of history. Political discourses, question and answer sessions, and public articulations are painstakingly created to pass on unambiguous messages and bring out wanted feelings.

The tone of political talk can either join together or partition a country. Pioneers who utilize comprehensive and positive language will generally cultivate a feeling of solidarity and fortitude among their constituents. On the other hand, fiery language and a troublesome tone can prompt polarization and social distress. The effect of political way of talking on open discernment is a demonstration of the force of language in forming cultural perspectives and ways of behaving.

Notwithstanding communicated in language, visual components, for example, non-verbal communication and looks add to the general tone of correspondence. Non-verbal signs frequently supplement or go against the expressed words, affecting how the message is gotten. A speaker's non-verbal communication, for example, can convey certainty, truthfulness, or anxiety, molding the audience's view of the message.

Social subtleties likewise assume a part in the effect of language and tone. Various societies might decipher similar words in an unexpected way, and what might be viewed as suitable in one social setting could be seen as hostile in another. Diverse correspondence expects aversion to these subtleties to stay away from misconceptions and advance compelling discourse.

The effect of language and tone isn't restricted to relational correspondence; it additionally stretches out to self-talk and inside exchange. The manner in which we address ourselves, the tone we use in our viewpoints, can fundamentally impact our psychological and close to home prosperity. Positive self-talk adds to fearlessness and flexibility, while negative self-talk can subvert confidence and add to pressure and nervousness.

Language and tone likewise assume a part in forming our view of the real world. The words we use to depict occasions or circumstances can impact how we and others see them. This peculiarity is apparent in media announcing, where the outlining of reports and the language utilized can shape popular assessment and impact cultural perspectives.

4.1 Exploring the nuances of language and its emotional impact

Language, as an intricate and dynamic arrangement of correspondence, serves as an instrument for passing on data as well as a vehicle for communicating feelings and molding human connections. The subtleties implanted inside language assume an essential part in deciding what messages are gotten and the profound mean for they convey. This investigation dives into the complicated aspects of language, disentangling its close to home profundity and analyzing the manners by which it impacts our insights, connections, and the more extensive cultural texture.

At its center, language is a flexible medium that permits people to verbalize considerations, share thoughts, and pass on data. In any case, past the surface degree of conveying realities, the selection of words and the construction of sentences add to the close to home reverberation of correspondence. Words are not simple vessels of data; they convey with them a range of feelings, going from satisfaction and sympathy to disappointment and outrage. The close to home effect of language not entirely set in stone by the unequivocal significance of words yet in addition by the setting in which they are utilized and the tone with which they are conveyed.

Consider, for example, the force of a straightforward "thank you." Past its superficial articulation of appreciation, the tone, pitch, and rhythm with which it is expressed can convey genuineness, warmth, or lack of interest. Also, the selection of words in communicating sympathies can either give solace or unintentionally create additional pain. The subtleties of language, subsequently, lie in the lexical implications of words as well as in the nuances of tone, pitch, and non-verbal signals.

In relational connections, language fills in as the essential vehicle for close to home association. The manner in which people express love, backing, or concern adds to the by and large profound tone of a relationship. Accomplices who speak with friendly and attesting language will quite often encourage closeness and re-inforce their bond. Running against the norm, connections described by unforgiving language or an absence of positive demeanor might confront difficulties in supporting close to home association.

In addition, the effect of language stretches out past expressed words to composed correspondence. In a time overwhelmed by computerized correspondence, instant messages, messages, and virtual entertainment presents have become necessary on our everyday collaborations.

The shortfall of eye to eye correspondence in composed text puts a more noteworthy accentuation on the selection of words and the tone passed on through them. An apparently harmless message can take on an alternate profound tint in light of the beneficiary's translation of the composed words.

In the advanced domain, emoticons and accentuation marks act as apparatuses for conveying tone and feeling. The incorporation of a smiley face can relax the effect of a message, while the shortfall of accentuation might be deciphered as easygoing or uninterested. The purposeful utilization of interjection imprints or capital letters can permeate a feeling of energy or earnestness. In that capacity, the profound effect of composed language isn't exclusively subject to the lexical substance yet is funda-mentally impacted by the visual and logical components going with the words.

Past individual connections, language assumes an essential part in molding the profound environment of networks and social orders. Public talk, political manner of speaking, and media stories add to the aggregate close to home insight of a general population. The words utilized by pioneers, policymakers, and power-houses can possibly motivate trust, solidarity, or, on the other hand, to impel dread, division, and enmity.

Political talks, for instance, are fastidiously created to inspire explicit profound reactions from the crowd. Pioneers influence language to verbalize a dream, rally backing, or address concerns. The close to home effect of political talk can impact general assessment, shape cultural perspectives, and even effect the course of history. The force of a powerful discourse lies in the consistent contentions introduced as well as in the close to home harmonies it strikes.

Likewise, media stories add to the close to home scene of a general public. The outlining of reports, the decision of language in titles, and the depiction of occasions can shape public discernment and impact close to home reactions. Sensationalized or one-sided language can set off dread, outrage, or nervousness, influencing the aggregate close to home prosperity of a local area. Then again, mindful and adjusted news coverage can possibly encourage grasping, sympathy, and informed direction.

Social subtleties further add layers of intricacy to the close to home effect of language. Various societies might credit changing close to home undertones to similar words or articulations. What might be seen as pleasant and aware in one culture could be deciphered as far off or contemptible in another. Diverse correspondence expects aversion to these subtleties to stay away from mistaken assumptions and cultivate viable exchange.

Besides, language isn't just a device for communicating feelings yet additionally a vehicle for exploring and managing them. The area of brain science perceives the significance of language in close to home articulation and guideline.

People who have a rich close to home jargon, able to do exactly articulating their sentiments, will quite often explore personal difficulties all the more really. Going against the norm, the people who battle to communicate their feelings in words might find it hard to impart their requirements and encounters.

The effect of language on close to home guideline is obvious in restorative settings. Psychotherapy frequently includes verbal articulation for of investigating and handling feelings. The specialist client discourse turns into a space where people can verbalize their considerations and sentiments, prompting expanded mindfulness and profound knowledge. The helpful utilization of language stretches out past verbal articulation to incorporate procedures like mental rebuilding, where people figure out how to reexamine pessimistic considerations and stories.

Moreover, the connection among language and feeling is bidirectional. While language fills in as a device for communicating feelings, feelings, thus, impact language use. Profound states can shape the selection of words, the manner of speaking, and the in general open style. For example, an individual encountering outrage might be more disposed to utilize fierce language, while somebody in a mindset of delight might communicate their thoughts with energy and energy.

The effect of language on feelings isn't bound to the domain of human correspondence. Research in the field of semantics and mental science investigates the manners by which language shapes mental cycles and close to home encounters. The Sapir-Whorf speculation, for example, proposes that language reflects as well as impacts suspected designs. The words accessible in a language might shape the manner in which people see and classify their close to home encounters.

Neuroscientific studies give bits of knowledge into the brain relates of language and feeling. Language handling and profound handling share brain processes, showing a perplexing transaction between the two. Cerebrum imaging studies uncover that the amygdala, a key locale engaged with close to home handling, is initiated during the experience of feelings as well as while handling sincerely loaded language. This cross-over highlights the close association among language and the profound cerebrum.

Notwithstanding the effect on people and networks, language assumes a huge part in forming social stories and memory. The tales we tell, the fantasies we spread, and the verifiable stories we build add to the social personality of a general public. The profound reverberation installed inside these accounts impacts how people see their social legacy and aggregate memory.

Language, hence, turns into an instrument for social safeguarding and transmission. The profound weight conveyed by social stories is gone down through ages, forming the qualities, convictions, and character of a local area.

The selection of words in portraying verifiable occasions, for example, can bring out pride, disgrace, or versatility, impacting the aggregate close to home cognizance of a general public.

In the domain of writing, writers tackle the force of language to make vivid profound encounters for perusers. The utilization of distinct language, illustrations, and story procedures permits writing to inspire a large number of feelings, moving perusers into the profound scenes of characters and universes. Whether through the endearing exposition of a romantic tale or the holding pressure of a thrill ride, writing turns into a mode for investigating the profundities of human inclination.

Verse, specifically, is prestigious for its capacity to distil complex feelings into language that reverberates on a close to home level. Writers utilize similitude, musicality, and imagery to convey the indescribable parts of human experience. The close to home effect of verse lies in the significance of the words as well as in the tasteful and musical characteristics that bring out an instinctive reaction.

4.2 Choosing the right tone for different audiences and contexts

The craft of correspondence reaches out past the simple choice of words; it incorporates the nuanced utilization of tone — a basic component that can shape how a message is gotten and deciphered. The significance of picking the right tone is especially obvious in different expert and individual settings, where successful correspondence depends on the clearness of the message as well as on its close to home reverberation with the target group.

In proficient settings, the capacity to observe and utilize the proper tone is an expertise that can fundamentally influence one's prosperity. Whether it's a business show, a client meeting, or an email trade, the tone utilized in correspondence makes way for viable coordinated effort and relationship-building. A misinterpreted tone can prompt errors, stressed connections, and even thwart proficient advancement.

Consider, for instance, the tone utilized in a business show. An excessively formal and inflexible tone could make a feeling of distance between the speaker and the crowd, possibly estranging them. Then again, a tone that is too relaxed or casual might be seen as amateurish, subverting the validity of the moderator. Finding some kind of harmony, embracing a tone that is both expert and drawing in, is vital in catching the crowd's consideration and passing on the message successfully.

In composed correspondence, for example, messages and reports, the tone turns out to be much more basic. The shortfall of non-verbal signals in composed text puts a more noteworthy accentuation on the words picked and the tone conveyed.

An ineffectively phrased email with an inadvertently cruel tone can prompt clash, while a painstakingly created message with a discretionary tone can encourage positive coordinated effort. Understanding the assumptions and inclinations of the beneficiary is critical to fitting the tone suitably.

Besides, the tone in proficient correspondence reaches out past convention; it likewise envelops components of compassion and thought. For instance, conveying valuable criticism in a steady and empowering tone can improve its viability. On the other hand, a basic or contemptuous tone might prompt protectiveness and opposition. Pioneers who excel at conveying input with a helpful and sympathetic tone cultivate a positive work culture where development and improvement are empowered.

In client communications, understanding the tone that reverberates with the specific client is vital. A few clients might favor a more formal and organized correspondence style, while others might see the value in a more loose and charming methodology. Adjusting the tone to line up with the client's inclinations improves the client experience as well as fortifies the expert relationship.

In the domain of client care, the tone utilized in settling issues and tending to worries assumes a crucial part in consumer loyalty. A responsive and compassionate tone can transform what is going on into an open door to exhibit incredible client care. On the other hand, a pretentious or pointless tone might heighten the issue and result in client disappointment. Organizations that focus on preparing their client support delegates in embracing a positive and compassionate tone frequently appreciate higher client maintenance and unwaveringness.

Past the expert circle, the significance of picking the right tone is similarly apparent in private connections. Whether in familial, heartfelt, or amicable settings, the tone utilized in correspondence can either support the relationship or make obstructions. Compelling correspondence inside private connections includes articulating one's thoughts obviously as well as figuring out the feelings of the other individual.

Consider the tone utilized in a heartfelt connection. Communicating affection, appreciation, and understanding in a warm and loving tone adds to the close to home association between accomplices. On the other hand, a basic or impassive tone can disintegrate the close to home security and lead to misconceptions. Accomplices who are sensitive to one another's close to home prompts and pick a steady tone construct a groundwork of trust and closeness.

In familial connections, the tone utilized in parent-kid correspondence altogether impacts the youngster's close to home turn of events. A sustaining and empowering tone cultivates a feeling that all is well with the world and self-esteem in youngsters.

Running against the norm, an unforgiving or belittling tone can affect a youngster's confidence. Guardians who perceive the effect of their tone on their youngsters' close to home prosperity endeavor to establish a correspondence climate that is both cherishing and valuable.

Fellowships, as well, blossom with powerful correspondence and the right tone. Steady and certifying language, combined with an uplifting vibe, reinforces the obligations of kinship. On the other hand, a negative or basic tone might strain the relationship and make distance. Companions who are aware of their tone add to a positive and improving correspondence dynamic.

The significance of tone in private connections stretches out to compromise. At the point when conflicts emerge, the tone utilized in resolving the issues can either work with goal or fuel strains. A discretionary and compassionate tone that looks to comprehend the other individual's viewpoint is bound to prompt productive exchange. Then again, a forceful or cautious tone might raise the contention and upset goal.

In instructive settings, the tone utilized by teachers significantly influences the opportunity for growth for understudies. A steady and empowering tone encourages a good homeroom climate where understudies feel inspired and esteemed. On the other hand, an unforgiving or decrying tone can make an unfriendly environment that blocks learning and dissolves understudies' certainty. Compelling teachers perceive the job of tone in establishing a helpful learning climate and endeavor to keep a positive and conscious correspondence style.

Understanding the subtleties of tone turns out to be considerably more critical in multifaceted correspondence. Various societies might ascribe differing close to home meanings to similar words or articulations. A tone that is seen as decisive and sure about one culture might be deciphered as self-important in another. Diverse communicators should be delicate to these subtleties to keep away from errors and construct compelling connections.

In the domain of public talking, the decision of tone is an essential component in drawing in and associating with the crowd. A speaker who embraces a tone that lines up with the crowd's assumptions and resounds with their feelings is bound to catch their consideration. Whether conveying an inspirational discourse, a convincing contention, or a useful show, speakers who excel at changing their tone to suit the specific circumstance and crowd improve the effect of their message.

The effect of tone isn't restricted to verbal correspondence; it stretches out to composed text in different structures, including writing, showcasing, and web-based entertainment. In writing, the tone set by the writer impacts the peruser's close to home insight. The utilization of spellbinding language, account style, and exchange add to the general tone of a scholarly work, bringing out unambiguous feelings and drenching the peruser in the story.

In showcasing, the tone utilized in publicizing and special materials assumes a huge part in forming buyer discernments. A brand that embraces a reliable and engaging tone in its informing lays out an unmistakable character and constructs profound associations with its crowd. The selection of words, symbolism, and generally speaking tone adds to the brand's character and impacts shopper steadfastness.

Online entertainment, with its unavoidable impact, is a stage where the effect of tone is intensified. The tone utilized in online entertainment posts, remarks, and connections can shape public discernment, trigger conversations, and even effect notorieties. People, associations, and individuals of note who are aware of their web-based tone explore the advanced scene all the more actually, encouraging positive commitment and relieving possible struggles.

4.3 The role of language in creating a memorable and lasting impression

Language, as a diverse device of correspondence, holds the ability to make permanent impressions that wait in the personalities of people. The shrewd utilization of words, whether spoken or composed, can possibly bring out feelings, shape insights, and leave an enduring engraving on memory. This investigation dives into the significant job of language in making vital encounters and getting through impressions across different areas of human association.

In the domain of public communicating in, the effect of language is especially articulated. A very much conveyed discourse, improved with persuasiveness and reverberation, can dazzle a group of people and implant the speaker's message in the aggregate memory. Extraordinary speakers since the beginning of time, from Martin Luther Ruler Jr's. "I Have a Fantasy" discourse to Winston Churchill's wartime addresses, epitomize the force of language to motivate, electrify, and make a persevering through imprint on the hearts and psyches of audience members.

The memorability of a discourse frequently pivots on the substance of the message as well as on the shrewd utilization of logical gadgets, striking symbolism, and the rhythm of language. The musical progression of words, combined with significant stops, can change a discourse into a critical encounter. Speakers who ace the subtleties of language, changing tone and speed to suit the profound tenor of their message, hoist their correspondence from simple transport of data to a full and remarkable experience.

Besides, narrating, inserted inside the texture of language, is an intense vehicle for making enduring impressions. Stories can summon sympathy, connect with the creative mind, and convey complex thoughts in an engaging way. The selection of words and the account structure add to the close to home effect of a story, making it critical and convincing. Whether in writing, film, or oral practices, stories persevere through time, carving themselves into the shared perspective.

In the field of promoting and publicizing, language assumes a significant part in forming brand character and making paramount missions. Infectious trademarks, paramount jingles, and convincing stories add to the close to home association among customers and brands. Notices that influence the force of language to summon humor, sentimentality, or goal have a more noteworthy probability of having an enduring effect in the personalities of the crowd. The language utilized in promoting materials turns into an essential piece of the brand's character, affecting customer discernments and driving brand dedication.

Past the domain of prearranged correspondence, unconstrained and valid language additionally holds the possibility to make essential impressions. In regular connections, people who have the capacity to articulate their thoughts with lucidity, earnestness, and a dash of moxy make a positive imprint on everyone around them. The specialty of discussion, improved by compelling relational abilities, includes the substance of the words as well as the tone, signals, and non-verbal prompts that add to the general impression.

In proficient settings, from new employee screenings to conferences, the job of language in forming discernments is vital. A very much created continue, an expressive introductory letter, and powerful verbal correspondence during interviews are parts of making a critical impact on likely bosses. The selection of words, the capacity to convey one's accomplishments and goals, and the general tone of correspondence impact how an individual is seen in the expert circle.

Initiative, as an indication of successful correspondence, depends vigorously on the capable utilization of language. Pioneers who can express a convincing vision, convey a feeling of direction, and motivate their groups through language make an enduring effect on hierarchical culture. The talks of extraordinary pioneers, like Steve Occupations or Nelson Mandela, represent how language can be an impetus for change, imparting an internal compass and leaving a getting through heritage.

In private connections, the effect of language on memory is clear in the trades between people. Articulations of adoration, consolation, and appreciation passed on through language add to the profound connections between relatives, companions, and significant others. On the other hand, terrible words or pessimistic language can leave scars on connections, highlighting the getting through effect of language in molding the close to home scene of special interactions.

The composed word, with its perpetual quality and openness, has an extraordinary ability to make enduring impressions. Writing, through its investigation of the human experience, has the ability to reverberate across time and societies. Books that well-spoken widespread insights, investigate significant bits of knowledge, or catch the outlook of a specific period become immortal, leaving an engraving on ages of perusers. The language utilized by artistic monsters, from Shakespeare to

Jane Austen, keeps on forming the abstract ordinance and impact the manner in which we see and decipher the world.

Verse, as a refined type of phonetic imaginativeness, epitomizes the capacity of language to make persevering through impressions. Writers distil complex feelings, perceptions, and reflections into a couple of painstakingly picked words, making a permanent imprint on the peruser's cognizance. The suggestive language, cadenced examples, and striking symbolism utilized in verse add to its memorability, permitting sections to wait in the personalities of perusers long after the words have been perused.

The job of language in memory reaches out to instructive settings, where successful educating includes the granting of data as well as the formation of paramount growth opportunities. Instructors who utilize connecting with language, intelligent showing techniques, and appealing models improve the maintenance of information. The utilization of language in instructive settings goes past conveying realities; it includes establishing a dynamic and animating climate that cultivates interest, decisive reasoning, and a long lasting adoration for learning.

In the advanced age, where data is spread through different web-based stages, the effect of language on memory is obvious in the domain of content creation. Whether through blog entries, web-based entertainment refreshes, or online articles, content makers who excel at creating convincing stories and eye catching titles have an enduring effect on their crowd. The language utilized in web-based content passes on data as well as shapes how data is gotten and recollected.

Web-based entertainment, with its quickness and instantaneousness, is a space where language can turn into a web sensation, making an aggregate memory that rises above individual encounters. Images, viral tweets, and effective hashtags embody how brief and sharp language can catch the general climate of a second and become carved into the social memory. The language utilized in web-based talk turns into a device for molding general assessment, starting developments, and impacting cultural perspectives.

The convergence of language and memory is likewise investigated in the field of mental science, where analysts look at what language procurement and use mean for memory processes. Studies recommend that the extravagance of language openness in youth adds to mental turn of events and memory development. Furthermore, bilingualism has been related with mental advantages, including upgraded memory and leader capabilities, featuring the mind boggling connection among language and mental cycles.

Neuroscientific examinations further enlighten the brain components associated with the transaction among language and memory. Mind imaging studies uncover the actuation of explicit cerebrum districts, for example, the hippocampus, during language handling and memory encoding. The interlacing of language and memory at the neurological level highlights the significant association between the two mental capabilities.

4.4 Practical exercises to enhance linguistic versatility

Etymological flexibility, the capacity to adjust and employ language successfully across different settings, is an important expertise that can fundamentally improve correspondence. Whether in proficient settings, social cooperations, or imaginative pursuits, people who have semantic adaptability are better prepared to explore different correspondence situations. This investigation digs into pragmatic activities intended to develop and improve etymological flexibility, enabling people to put themselves out there with lucidity, accuracy, and versatility.

Extend Your Jargon:

A rich and various jargon is the underpinning of semantic flexibility. Consistently integrating new words into your dictionary not just improves your capacity to communicate nuanced thoughts yet in addition permits you to fit your language to various crowds and circumstances. Participate in exercises like perusing books from different sorts, buying into expression of-the-day benefits, or keeping an individual jargon diary. Effectively involving new words in your everyday correspondence supports their maintenance and reconciliation into your etymological collection.

Practice Different Composing Styles:

Composing is a useful asset for sharpening semantic flexibility. Try different things with different composing styles, for example, influential, enlightening, innovative, and formal. Create expositions, brief tales, articles, and business messages to foster the capacity to adjust your composition to various purposes and crowds. Look for criticism from companions or coaches to refine your composing style, focusing on tone, clearness, and intelligibility.

Take part in Discussions and Conversations:

Taking part in discussions and conversations improves your skill to explain contentions, answer contradicting perspectives, and think and react quickly. Take part in conventional discussions or join conversation bunches where different points of view are supported. This improves your verbal relational abilities as well as opens you to various explanatory methodologies, assisting you with turning out to be more adroit at fitting your language to convince, illuminate, or arrange.

Investigate Various Types of Writing:

Writing offers a tremendous scene of etymological styles and story methods. Perusing works from different kinds opens you to fluctuated phonetic articulations, assisting you with valuing the subtleties of language. Investigate exemplary writing, contemporary fiction, verifiable, verse, and plays. Focus on the writer's decision of language, tone, and style, and consider how these components add to the general effect of the composition.

Submerge Yourself in Multilingual Conditions:

Openness to different dialects widens your semantic point of view and upgrades your versatility. In the event that conceivable, submerge yourself in multilingual conditions where you can notice and draw in with speakers of various dialects.

This openness advances how you might interpret language variety as well as gives experiences into social subtleties that impact correspondence.

Practice Unrehearsed Talking:

The capacity to talk unhesitatingly and soundly on the spot is a sign of semantic flexibility. Practice unrehearsed talking by picking arbitrary subjects and conveying short discourses or reactions. This exercise improves your skill to sort out considerations rapidly, adjust to surprising circumstances, and convey thoughts in an unmistakable and convincing way. Consider taking part in comedy exercises or improvised talking clubs to additionally refine this expertise.

Adjust Your Correspondence Style:

Various circumstances call for various correspondence styles. Work on adjusting your correspondence style in light of the specific situation, crowd, and reason. For instance, the language you use in a proper conference might vary from the language utilized in an easygoing get-together. Focus on the social and accepted practices of the setting and change your tone, convention, and selection of words appropriately.

Get and Integrate Criticism:

Request input on your correspondence style from friends, coaches, or language experts. Useful input gives important bits of knowledge into regions to progress, assisting you with refining your language abilities. Effectively integrate criticism into your correspondence practice, whether it relates to clearness, succinctness, or the propriety of your language in various settings.

Partake in Language Trades:

Language trades offer chances to associate with local speakers and work on your conversational abilities. Join language trade projects or stages where you can take part in discussions with people conversant in the language you are learning. This true practice opens you to casual articulations, social subtleties, and various correspondence styles, encouraging semantic flexibility.

Make and Present Multimodal Content:

Embrace assorted methods of correspondence by making sight and sound substance. Foster introductions, digital recordings, recordings, or infographics that pass on data utilizing a mix of visual, hear-able, and literary components. This exercise not just improves your capacity to pass messages on through various mediums yet in addition urges you to adjust your language to really suit every mode.

Investigate Territorial Vernaculars and Shoptalk:

Language adaptability incorporates a comprehension of provincial vernaculars and informal articulations. Look into the etymological subtleties of various districts, including territorial accents, shoptalk, and expressions. This information adds to your general language capability as well as empowers you to interface all the more really with people from different foundations.

Foster Multifaceted Relational abilities:

Multifaceted correspondence includes exploring assorted social standards, decorum, and correspondence styles. Effectively look for chances to connect with people from various social foundations. Go to comprehensive developments, join global gatherings, or take part in multifaceted correspondence studios. This openness upgrades your capacity to impart successfully in socially assorted settings, cultivating phonetic adaptability.

Investigate and Copy Different Speaking Styles:

Breaking down and emulating different talking styles is a successful method for assimilating assorted semantic examples. Watch discourses, meetings, or TED Talks conveyed by speakers with unmistakable correspondence styles. Focus on their selection of words, tone, pacing, and non-verbal signals. Work on integrating components of these styles into your own correspondence, permitting you to adjust your methodology in light of the ideal effect.

Use Pretending Situations:

Pretending situations recreate genuine circumstances and give a stage to rehearse language flexibility. Make situations pertinent to your own or proficient life, for example, new employee screenings, discussions, or social communications. Accept various jobs and work on adjusting your language to suit the unique situation, whether you are assuming the part of a questioner, client, or group pioneer.

Stay up to date with Phonetic Patterns:

Language is dynamic, with patterns and advancements persistently forming its scene. Remain informed about etymological patterns, arising words, and changes in correspondence styles. Follow language-related distributions, sites, and online entertainment accounts that talk about developing language designs. Remaining sensitive to phonetic patterns guarantees that your correspondence stays current and resounds with contemporary crowds.

Use Language Learning Applications:

Language learning applications offer intelligent and connecting with stages to improve etymological adaptability. Numerous applications give practices that attention on different parts of language, including jargon extension, elocution, and social subtleties. Integrate language learning applications into your everyday practice to support language abilities in a dynamic and open manner.

Participate in Elocution Practice:

Clear and exact elocution contributes fundamentally to powerful correspondence. Participate in elocution activities to refine your verbalization and sound. Utilize online assets, language learning stages, or language trade accomplices to rehearse elocution. Record yourself talking and contrast it with local speakers to distinguish regions for development.

Partake in Speakers or Public Speaking Gatherings:

Speakers Global and comparative public talking bunches give strong conditions to people to refine their talking and initiative abilities. Take part in these gatherings to acquire reasonable involvement with conveying discourses, getting productive criticism, and refining your public talking skills. The assorted scope of subjects and talking styles experienced in such gatherings adds to etymological flexibility.

Compose Across Various Classifications:

Composing across various kinds improves your flexibility in passing messages on through different styles. Explore different avenues regarding composing verse, fiction, true to life, business records, and specialized content. Every sort presents special phonetic difficulties and open doors, permitting you to develop a flexible composing style that can resound with different crowds.

Reflect and Repeat:

Standard reflection on your language use is essential to the course of progress. Subsequent to participating in phonetic activities or correspondence situations, carve out opportunity to consider your presentation. Distinguish regions where you succeeded and regions for development. Put forth unambiguous objectives for upgrading phonetic adaptability, and iteratively refine your language abilities in light of your appearance and criticism.

Creating etymological flexibility is a continuous interaction that includes a blend of purposeful practice, openness to different language settings, and an eagerness to adjust. The commonsense activities framed above give an establishment to developing etymological flexibility, however there are extra techniques and exercises that people can integrate into their language improvement venture. This lengthy investigation digs further into the subtleties of phonetic adaptability and presents a variety of activities to additional upgrade this significant ability.

Investigate Multilingual Writing:

Dig into writing written in different dialects to acquire openness to assorted semantic styles. This can incorporate works deciphered from different dialects or those written in bilingual or multilingual configurations. Perusing writing in various dialects offers bits of knowledge into social subtleties, phonetic articulations, and narrating strategies that add to etymological flexibility.

Examine Discourse Examples in Web recordings:

Digital broadcasts give an abundance of different substance and proposition a valuable chance to examine different discourse designs. Pay attention to webcasts that cover a scope of themes and incorporate speakers with particular correspondence styles. Focus on inflection, pacing, and jargon decisions. Consider impersonating parts of these discourse examples to grow your phonetic collection.

Participate in Unpremeditated Talking:

Impromptu talking, or talking without earlier planning, is a significant activity for creating phonetic flexibility. Pick an irregular subject and challenge yourself to talk intelligibly and powerfully on the spot. This exercise improves your skill to think and react quickly, adjust your language to the circumstance, and impart thoughts actually progressively.

Make Multilingual Cheat sheets:

Grow your jargon in numerous dialects by making cheat sheets that component words, expressions, and articulations from various phonetic foundations. Utilize these cheat sheets for customary survey, integrating them into your everyday language learning schedule. This exercise upgrades your jargon as well as builds up your capacity to consistently switch between dialects.

Direct Near Language Investigation:

Select a subject or topic and investigate the way things are examined in various dialects. Lead a relative examination of how subtleties, social references, and colloquialisms fluctuate across dialects. This exercise cultivates an appreciation for the social and phonetic variety intrinsic in correspondence, adding to a more nuanced and versatile way to deal with language use.

Take part in Recreated Culturally diverse Situations:

Recreate multifaceted situations to work on adjusting your language to various social settings. Pretend situations where social standards, correspondence styles, and assumptions change. This exercise upgrades your multifaceted relational abilities, permitting you to explore different social settings with awareness and versatility.

Explore different avenues regarding Transcreation:

Transcreation includes adjusting content starting with one language then onto the next while keeping up with its expected significance, tone, and style. Practice transcreation by taking a piece of composing, a sonnet, or a melody verse and adjusting it into another dialect. This exercise levels up your interpretation abilities as well as develops how you might interpret semantic subtleties.

Take part in Language Submersion Projects:

Language drenching programs give an escalated climate to language learning. Take part in submersion programs where the objective language is spoken broadly. Whether through language submersion courses, concentrate on abroad projects, or language-serious travel encounters, inundation speeds up your capacity to adjust to various semantic settings.

Make a Language Learning Online journal:

Begin a blog committed to your language learning venture. Compose posts in the dialects you are getting the hang of, sharing your encounters, difficulties, and progress. Draw in with language learning networks and look for criticism on your composition. This exercise upgrades your composing abilities as well as makes a stage for social trade and language investigation.

Use Computer generated Reality Language Learning:

Investigate augmented reality (VR) language learning stages that reproduce certifiable language situations. VR innovation permits you to collaborate with symbols, take part in virtual discussions, and explore language-rich conditions. This vivid methodology speeds up language obtaining and opens you to different etymological circumstances.

Partake in Language Meetup Gatherings:

Go to language meetup gatherings or language trade occasions in your neighborhood local area or on the web. These social occasions furnish chances to rehearse dialects with local speakers, get quick input, and notice different conversational styles. Language meetups encourage a steady climate for semantic investigation and social trade.

Join Composing Studios in Various Kinds:

Grow your composing abilities by partaking in studios that emphasis on various kinds. Whether it's fiction, verse, news-casting, or specialized composition, every type presents remarkable semantic difficulties. Taking part in assorted composing studios opens you to different composing styles, assisting you with adjusting your language to various types of articulation.

Try different things with Code-Exchanging:

Code-exchanging includes shifting back and forth between at least two dialects inside a solitary discussion. Practice code-exchanging in a controlled way, purposely integrating components of various dialects into your discourse or composing. This exercise improves your capacity to explore multilingual conditions and adjust your language to various questioners.

Go to Multilingual Exhibitions:

Go to exhibitions, like plays, shows, or verbally expressed word occasions, where different dialects are utilized. Encountering language in a performative setting opens you to the expressive and emotive elements of etymological flexibility. Focus on how entertainers use language to bring out feelings and connect with the crowd.

Add to Multilingual Internet based Stages:

Draw in with online stages that help multilingual substance creation. Contribute articles, remarks, or conversations in various dialects on stages that take care of a different crowd. This exercise refines your language abilities as well as interfaces you with people from around the world, cultivating a worldwide point of view on phonetic flexibility.

Interpret Multilingual Texts:

Work on interpreting texts that include numerous dialects. This could incorporate interpreting writing, tune verses, or interactive media content that integrates different etymological components. Interpreting multilingual texts levels up your interpretation abilities and develops how you might interpret how dialects converge and impact one another.

Investigate Language Development and Neologisms:

Research how dialects advance over the long haul and adjust to cultural changes. Concentrate on the presentation of new words, articulations, and neologisms. Remain informed about semantic patterns, including the reception of words from various dialects. This exercise guarantees that your language abilities remain receptive to contemporary use and social movements.

Use Discourse Acknowledgment Programming:

Explore different avenues regarding discourse acknowledgment programming that gives input on elocution, sound, and clearness. This innovation assists you with refining your communicated in language abilities and adjust your elocution to various accents. Normal utilization of discourse acknowledgment devices improves your oral correspondence capability across different phonetic settings.

Make Language Learning Difficulties:

Set language learning difficulties that urge you to investigate various parts of phonetic adaptability. For instance, challenge yourself to compose a sonnet in a language you are learning, give a show on a complicated subject, or participate in a discussion with a language trade accomplice. These difficulties give organized open doors to ability improvement.

Look for Criticism from Local Speakers:

Effectively look for input on your language abilities from local speakers. Local speakers can give bits of knowledge into social subtleties, colloquial articulations, and unobtrusive semantic subtleties that might get away from non-local speakers. Valuable input from local speakers is priceless for refining your language use and guaranteeing realness.

Chapter 5

Public Speaking Techniques

Public talking is an expertise that holds huge importance in different parts of life. Whether you are tending to a huge crowd, introducing a proposition to a client, or in any event, partaking in an easygoing gathering conversation, viable public talking can enormously affect your capacity to pass on your message convincingly and have an enduring effect. In this extensive investigation of public talking procedures, we will dig into the key components that add to dominance in this fine art, going from readiness and conveyance to conquering nervousness and drawing in your crowd.

At the center of fruitful public talking lies exhaustive arrangement. The significance of realizing your material couldn't possibly be more significant. Start by completely exploring your theme, gathering significant data, and sorting out it in a sensible succession. This not just improves how you might interpret the topic yet additionally imparts trust in your capacity to resolve any inquiries that might emerge. As you coordinate your substance, guarantee that it follows an intelligent construction, with a reasonable presentation, body, and end. This design furnishes your crowd with a guide, making it more straightforward for them to follow and fathom your message.

While setting up your discourse, consider your crowd's degree of understanding and interest in the point. Tailor your substance to reverberate with your crowd, utilizing language and models that are engaging to them.

This approach dazzles your audience members as well as lays out an association among you and the crowd. Furthermore, be aware of the time designated for your discourse and work on conveying your message inside that time span. Using time productively is a pivotal part of public talking, as surpassing the dispensed time can bring about separation from the crowd.

When your material is coordinated, shift your concentration to the conveyance of your discourse. One of the best methods to catch your crowd's consideration is through a convincing opening. Begin with a strong statement, an interesting inquiry, or a dazzling story that establishes the vibe for your show. A solid opening gets consideration as well as lays out a positive initial feeling, establishing the groundwork for a fruitful discourse.

Non-verbal communication assumes an essential part in successful correspondence. Keep up with great stance, visually engage, and use motions to underline central issues. Your non-verbal communication ought to pass on certainty and energy, building up the message you are conveying verbally. Try not to occupy developments or characteristics that might take away from your validity. Practice your non-verbal communication during practices to guarantee that it supplements your discourse and improves your general conveyance.

Notwithstanding non-verbal communication, vocal assortment is one more basic component of viable correspondence. Balance your voice to underscore significant focuses, fluctuate your pitch and speed to keep up with interest, and use stops decisively to permit your crowd to ingest key data. A dull conveyance can prompt withdrawal, so endeavor to implant energy and excitement into your voice.

A critical part of fruitful public talking is the capacity to adjust to the requirements of your crowd. Be receptive to their responses and change your conveyance likewise. Assuming that you sense that your crowd is losing interest, consider infusing humor or offering a provocative conversation starter to reconnect them. Adaptability and responsiveness to your crowd's signals add to a more unique and effective show.

One more remarkable procedure to upgrade your public talking abilities is the utilization of visuals. Visual guides like slides, outlines, and charts can really supplement your verbal message, making complex data more open to your crowd. In any case, it is crucial for use visuals sensibly and guarantee that they improve, as opposed to eclipse, your verbal correspondence. Work on integrating visuals into your show to flawlessly incorporate them with your discourse.

Overseeing apprehension is quite difficult for some speakers. In any case, as opposed to survey anxiety as an obstruction, consider it as energy that can be directed into your show. To ease apprehension, practice profound breathing activities and envision a positive result. Moreover, find out about the setting before your show to lessen the component of the unexplored world.

Recall that apprehension is a characteristic reaction, and, surprisingly, experienced speakers experience it. Embrace the apprehensive energy and use it to fuel a dynamic and connecting with conveyance.

Practice is a basic part of improving your public talking abilities. Practice your whole discourse on various occasions, zeroing in on both substance and conveyance. Practices permit you to refine your message, distinguish regions that might require explanation, and clean your conveyance. Practice before a mirror to notice your non-verbal communication and looks, or record yourself to equitably investigate your presentation. Request input from confided in partners or coaches to acquire significant experiences and make essential changes.

Integrate input into your practice interaction to refine your show consistently. Focus on pacing, clearness of articulation, and by and large soundness. As you become more acquainted with your material, your certainty will normally expand, adding to a more cleaned and guaranteed conveyance.

Compelling public talking stretches out past the expressed word; it incorporates the craft of tuning in also. Be mindful of your crowd's responses and be ready to change your message in view of their criticism. Energize questions and connection, cultivating a dynamic and drawing in return with your crowd. Undivided attention not just upgrades your capacity to answer your crowd yet in addition exhibits regard for their feedback.

One frequently disregarded part of public talking is the force of narrating. Meshing important stories and accounts into your discourse adds a human touch, making your message more interesting and significant. Stories can bring out feelings, catch consideration, and commute home central issues. Consider integrating individual tales or genuine models that resound with your crowd, upgrading the effect of your message.

Keeping a positive mentality is urgent for compelling public talking. Center around the worth of your message and the chance to share information or move others. Shift your mentality from hesitance to crowd centeredness, underscoring the significance of your message to those tuning in. Perception strategies can be strong in developing a positive mentality; envision yourself conveying an effective and significant show.

Tending to and beating public talking nervousness is a typical test. Begin by recognizing that apprehension is a characteristic reaction and reevaluating it as a wellspring of energy as opposed to an impediment. Foster an everyday practice of unwinding works out, like profound breathing and representation, to quiet your nerves prior to talking. Slowly open yourself to talking open doors, beginning with more modest gatherings and advancing to bigger crowds. Each fruitful experience assembles certainty and adds to beating nervousness.

Successful utilization of humor can be an important device out in the open talking. Humor eases up the mind-set, draws in the crowd, and makes an association between the speaker and audience members. In any case, it is vital for use humor sensibly and guarantee that it lines up with the specific situation and tone of your message. Be aware of social responsive qualities and keep away from humor that might be disruptive or hostile. Work on integrating humor into your discourse to check its effect and refine your conveyance.

Drawing in your crowd is a crucial objective of public talking. Encourage an association by tending to your crowd straightforwardly, utilizing comprehensive language, and recognizing their point of view. Empower investment through questions, surveys, or intuitive exercises that include the crowd. At the point when audience members feel effectively involved, they are bound to hold and assimilate your message. Consider the inclinations and assumptions for your crowd while planning intelligent components to guarantee pertinence and adequacy.

The specialty of influence is firmly interwoven with public talking. To convince your crowd, obviously articulate the advantages or outcomes of your message and give supporting proof. Utilize convincing language and appeal to feelings to summon a reaction. Expect likely complaints and address them proactively, supporting the believability of your message. Making an influential message requires a profound comprehension of your crowd and the capacity to tailor your contentions to resound with their qualities and convictions.

Integrating visual guides into your show can essentially upgrade the effect of your message. Visuals give a visual portrayal of key data, making it more straightforward for the crowd to understand complex ideas. Use slides, diagrams, or charts to supplement your verbal message and make a multi-modular growth opportunity. Nonetheless, it is urgent to utilize visuals sparingly and guarantee that they improve, instead of occupy from, your verbally expressed words. Work on synchronizing your verbal and visual components to make a consistent and firm show.

Successful public talking stretches out past the stage or platform; it envelops the capacity to impart unhesitatingly in different settings. Whether you are in a conference, a systems administration occasion, or a relaxed discussion, the standards of public talking stay material. Focus on your non-verbal communication, vocal tone, and generally attitude to convey certainty and validity. Work on articulating your contemplations obviously and succinctly in various settings to fabricate flexibility in your relational abilities.

The force of quiet ought to be acknowledged with a sober mind openly talking. Key stops permit your crowd to ingest central issues, underline significant thoughts, and make a feeling of expectation. Work on integrating stops into your discourse to upgrade its mood and effect. Keep away from the compulsion to fill each second with words, as snapshots of quietness can be amazing assets for accentuating and interspersing your message.

Building affinity with your crowd is fundamental for powerful correspondence. Lay out an association by communicating realness and appeal. Share applicable individual encounters or experiences that reverberate with your crowd's advantages or difficulties. Showing weakness and transparency cultivates a feeling of association and urges your crowd to connect all the more profoundly with your message. Endeavor to make a conversational tone that welcomes audience members into a discourse instead of a speech.

Understanding the social setting of your crowd is vital for compelling correspondence. Be aware of social subtleties, inclinations, and responsive qualities that might affect your message. Adjust your correspondence style and content to line up with the social assumptions for your crowd. Develop a multifaceted mindfulness that empowers you to interface with different crowds and impart in a manner that is deferential and comprehensive.

Innovation has turned into a necessary piece of present day correspondence, and its viable use can improve your public talking endeavors. Dive more deeply into show devices, general media gear, and virtual stages to guarantee a consistent conveyance. Work on involving innovation ahead of time to limit the gamble of specialized errors and disturbances. Influence innovation to draw in your crowd through intelligent components, virtual surveys, or mixed media introductions.

The specialty of public talking stretches out past individual articulation; it includes the capacity to work with significant conversations and draw in a different crowd. Develop successful help abilities by empowering interest, overseeing overall vibes, and establishing a cooperative climate. Use inquiries without a right or wrong answer to invigorate conversation and welcome different viewpoints. Dominating help improves your capacity to associate with your crowd and make an intelligent and dynamic talking experience.

Productive criticism is an important device for constant improvement out in the open talking. Look for criticism from confided in partners, guides, or friends to acquire bits of knowledge into your assets and regions for advancement. Embrace criticism as a chance for development and refinement. Effectively carry out helpful ideas to upgrade your conveyance, content, and in general viability as a public speaker.

Public talking isn't restricted to prearranged discourses; off the cuff talking is an important expertise that can be sharpened through training. Foster the capacity to express your considerations plainly and succinctly on the spot. Practice improvised talking in different settings to fabricate certainty and flexibility. Embrace the test of reasoning on your feet and answering successfully to surprising circumstances.

Successful utilization of visual guides is an expertise that can essentially improve your public talking influence. Make outwardly engaging slides or show materials that help your message. Guarantee that visuals are clear, brief, and line up with the general topic of your discourse.

Practice flawlessly coordinating visual components into your show to make a strong and drawing in experience for your crowd.

Keeping up with validness is a foundation of significant public talking. Be certifiable in offering your viewpoints, convictions, and feelings. Credibility cultivates an association with your crowd and lays out trust. Try not to take on a persona that feels inauthentic, as it can dissolve believability and reduce the effect of your message. Embrace your one of a kind voice and point of view, permitting it to radiate through in your public talking tries.

Public talking is a developing expertise that can be ceaselessly refined and extended. Go to studios, workshops, or preparing projects to keep up to date with the most recent patterns and strategies openly talking. Network with different speakers, trade bits of knowledge, and gain from their encounters. Embrace a mentality of deep rooted figuring out how to constantly upgrade your capability and adjust to the developing scene of public talking.

Building major areas of strength for a presence is progressively important in the computerized age, and it stretches out to public talking too. Influence online entertainment stages, online classes, and virtual talking potential chances to contact a worldwide crowd. Adjust your show style to suit virtual settings, integrating drawing in visuals, intuitive components, and innovation to upgrade the web based talking experience. Develop a convincing web-based persona that lines up with your message and reverberates with different crowds.

Public talking is certainly not a single undertaking; cooperation and systems administration are key parts of progress. Draw in with individual speakers, occasion coordinators, and industry experts to grow your organization. Team up on projects, share experiences, and investigate open doors for joint talking commitment. Organizing opens ways to new open doors as well as enhances your viewpoint and information in the field of public talking.

Successful correspondence is a two-way road, and undivided attention is a necessary part. Focus on the verbal and non-verbal signals of your crowd, permitting you to check their degree of commitment and understanding. Urge questions and input to make a discourse that upgrades common comprehension. The capacity to listen effectively and answer mindfully adds to a more unique and significant public talking experience.

The force of compassion couldn't possibly be more significant openly talking. Grasp the points of view, concerns, and interests of your crowd to really tailor your message. Recognize and approve the feelings and encounters of your audience members, making an association that rises above the verbally expressed word. Exhibiting compassion cultivates a positive and comprehensive talking climate, upgrading the general effect of your message.

Developing flexibility is fundamental for exploring the difficulties and misfortunes that might emerge in the domain of public talking. Few out of every odd show will unfurl impeccably, and unexpected hindrances might happen. Foster flexibility by review difficulties as any open doors for development, gaining from misfortunes, and keeping a positive mentality. Strength empowers you to quickly return from difficulties and keep developing as a certain and compelling public speaker.

5.1 Overcoming fear and anxiety associated with public speaking

Public talking is a typical trepidation that numerous people wrestle with, frequently positioning higher than the feeling of dread toward death in different overviews. The uneasiness related with talking before a group of people can be overpowering, prompting anxiety, self-question, and a scope of actual side effects. Defeating dread and tension openly talking requires a mix of mental systems, down to earth procedures, and reliable practice.

Understanding the main drivers of public talking tension is a vital initial phase in conquering it. Feeling of dread toward judgment, dismissal, or humiliation can set off nervousness for some speakers. Furthermore, worries about failing to remember the substance, staggering over words, or confronting surprising inquiries add to the general fear. Distinguishing explicit apprehensions permits people to address them all the more really and execute designated methodologies for defeating uneasiness.

One compelling methodology for conquering public talking tension is orderly desensitization. This approach includes slowly presenting oneself to the dreaded circumstance in a controlled and bit by bit way. Begin with low-nervousness circumstances, like talking before a little and strong gathering of companions or family. As solace and certainty develop, dynamically increment the intricacy of the talking circumstances, progressively moving towards bigger crowds. This methodical openness assists people with building strength and diminish uneasiness over the long haul.

Positive perception is a strong method that includes intellectually practicing a fruitful talking experience. Before a talking commitment, find opportunity to picture yourself talking unhesitatingly and really. Envision the positive responses from the crowd and the feeling of achievement that follows. Representation makes a positive outlook, supporting the conviction that effective results are conceivable as well as feasible.

Care and unwinding methods can fundamentally mitigate public talking uneasiness. Rehearsing profound breathing activities, contemplation, or moderate muscle unwinding helps quiet the sensory system and diminishes the actual side effects of uneasiness, like shudder hands or a hustling heartbeat. Integrating these methods into a pre-discourse routine can make a feeling of centeredness and control, making it simpler to oversee nervousness during the genuine show.

Mental rebuilding is a restorative procedure that includes testing and changing negative idea designs. Recognize and challenge unreasonable contemplations connected with public talking, like horrendous reasoning or excessively regrettable self-talk. Supplant these considerations with additional reasonable and positive attestations. For instance, rather than thinking, "I'll humiliate myself," supplant it with "I'm completely ready, and I can deal with this show." Over the long haul, mental rebuilding helps shift the outlook from one of dread to one of certainty.

Public talking courses and studios give an organized climate to people to create and rehearse their talking abilities. These courses frequently incorporate open doors for members to convey discourses, get valuable criticism, and progressively construct trust in a strong setting. Joining a public talking gathering or club, for example, Speakers, offers a local area of similar people who share comparable difficulties and objectives. Customary cooperation in such gatherings considers nonstop practice and criticism, cultivating both expertise improvement and certainty.

Readiness is a critical calculate decreasing nervousness related with public talking. Completely research and sort out your substance, guaranteeing an unmistakable construction and intelligent stream. Practice your discourse on numerous occasions, finding out more about the material and refining your conveyance. The more pre-arranged you are, the more certain you will feel while confronting a crowd of people. Furthermore, being good to go goes about as a support against startling difficulties, adding to a feeling of control.

Experience with the talking climate can fundamentally decrease nervousness. Visit the scene ahead of time, if conceivable, to get to know the format, acoustics, and specialized gear. Stand on the stage or at the platform to figure out the space. Knowledge of the environmental factors kills the component of the obscure, causing the genuine show to feel more great and reasonable.

Public talking nervousness frequently shows genuinely, with side effects like a dashing heart, unsteady hands, or tense muscles. Actual activity is a characteristic method for reducing pressure and uneasiness. Take part in standard active work to deliver developed strain and advance a feeling of prosperity. Whether it's a lively walk, an exercise, or yoga, integrating actual activity into your routine can decidedly affect both your psychological and actual state, adding to generally speaking tension decrease.

Rehearsing before a believed companion or relative can be a useful method for mimicking the experience of talking before a crowd of people. Demand productive criticism on your substance, conveyance, and by and large show. This training crowd can give important experiences and support, assisting you with refining your exhibition and fabricate certainty. Continuously increment the size of your training crowd to emulate different talking situations.

A typical trepidation in broad daylight talking is failing to remember the substance or staggering over words. To address this, emphasis on central issues and utilize visual guides or notes as prompts. Separate your discourse into more modest areas and practice each section autonomously. By dominating more modest parts, you construct trust in your capacity to review and understandable the substance. Furthermore, taking on a conversational tone can cause the conveyance to feel more normal, diminishing the probability of stalling out on unambiguous words or expressions.

Understand that committing errors is a characteristic piece of public talking. Rather than survey botches as disappointments, consider them to be amazing open doors for development and improvement. Crowds are by and large sympathetic, and they comprehend that speakers are human. Embrace defects and use them as opportunities for growth. After some time, a seriously tolerating mentality towards errors can fundamentally diminish uneasiness and increment flexibility out in the open talking circumstances.

Fostering major areas of strength for a with the crowd is a strong method for defeating tension. Instead of zeroing in internal on private feelings of dread, shift the concentration to the message you need to pass on and the effect it can have on your crowd. Consider the worth you bring to your audience members and the information or motivation you can share. Moving the concentrate outward diverts anxious energy towards making a significant association with the crowd.

Rethinking nervousness as fervor is a mental strategy that includes changing the understanding of physiological reactions. Rather than naming the anxious sentiments as nervousness, decipher them as a characteristic reaction to the fervor of sharing important data. Embracing the energy related with fervor can change uneasiness into a positive power that fills a dynamic and drawing in show. This change in discernment permits speakers to channel apprehensive energy into excitement and enthusiasm for their message.

Public talking nervousness frequently comes from the apprehension about being judged or adversely assessed by others. To neutralize this trepidation, take on a mentality that spotlights on the crowd's requirements and interests as opposed to on private worries. Consider the worth of your message and how it can help your audience members. At the point when the center movements from reluctance to crowd centeredness, the tension reduces, and speakers can move toward the show with a feeling of direction and association.

Self-sympathy is an essential part of conquering public talking uneasiness. Indulge yourself with benevolence and understanding, recognizing that talking in broad daylight is a difficult undertaking for some. Perceive that committing errors or confronting difficulties doesn't lessen your value. Practice self-caring self-talk and stay away from cruel self-analysis. Developing self-empathy establishes a more strong inward climate, lessening uneasiness and cultivating a positive outlook.

Building a progressive openness order is an organized way to deal with methodicallly face and defeat public talking fears. Start by taking part in low-nervousness talking circumstances, like addressing a little gathering of companions. As solace and certainty increment, continuously open yourself to additional difficult circumstances, pursuing bigger crowds or more proper settings. This bit by bit approach takes into consideration a steady desensitization to the feeling of dread toward public talking, building strength en route.

The apprehension about open talking is much of the time established in the expectation of adverse results. To neutralize this expectation, center around sure attestations and imagine effective talking encounters. Make a psychological picture of yourself talking unhesitatingly and getting positive input from the crowd. Build up the conviction that positive results are conceivable as well as likely. Positive perception makes a productive outlook that adds to expanded certainty and decreased tension.

Steady self-talk is an integral asset in beating public talking tension. Supplant negative or self-decisive considerations with positive and empowering articulations. For instance, supplant "I'll screw up and humiliate myself" with "I'm completely ready, and I can deal with this." Work on developing a positive internal discourse to construct self-assurance and neutralize uneasiness prompting considerations. Steady sure self-talk supports a tough and enabled mentality.

Joining a public talking bunch, like Speakers, gives a steady local area to people hoping to beat their anxiety toward public talking. These gatherings offer an organized climate for rehearsing and refining talking abilities.

5.2 Body language and non-verbal communication tips

Non-verbal communication and non-verbal correspondence are fundamental parts of viable relational correspondence. The manner in which we move, signal, and communicate our thoughts non-verbally can pass on an abundance of data, frequently molding the general effect of our messages. Understanding and dominating non-verbal communication can fundamentally upgrade our capacity to associate with others, construct affinity, and convey certainty. In this extensive investigation, we will dive into key non-verbal communication and non-verbal correspondence tips that can be applied across different settings.

1. **Keep up with Positive Stance:**

   Great stance is the groundwork of solid non-verbal communication. Stand or sit upright, with your shoulders back and your chest open. Try not to slump or folding your arms, as these signals can convey protectiveness or lack of engagement. Positive stance improves your actual presence as well as conveys certainty and commitment to people around you.

2. **Visually connect:**

   Eye to eye connection is a strong non-verbal signal that lays out an association between people. While talking or tuning in, keep in touch to convey mindfulness and truthfulness. Abstain from gazing eagerly, as this can be seen as forceful. Finding some kind of harmony with eye to eye connection encourages a feeling of trust and commitment to your cooperations.

3. **Utilize Open Motions:**

   Signals are a characteristic and expressive piece of correspondence. Utilize open and deliberate signals to supplement your verbal messages. Abstain from folding your arms or taking on shut off motions, as these can make a boundary among you and your crowd. Open motions convey transparency, energy, and validness.

4. **Mind Your Looks:**

   Looks assume a critical part in conveying feelings and expectations. Be aware of your looks, guaranteeing they line up with the message you need to pass on. Grin really to communicate warmth and agreeability. Try not to glare or showing articulations that might be confused. A very much controlled and expressive face upgrades your by and large non-verbal correspondence.

5. **Change Your Tone and Pitch:**

   Non-verbal correspondence stretches out to vocal components like tone and pitch. Tweak your voice to convey accentuation and feeling. A shifted vocal tone catches consideration and adds subtlety to your verbally expressed words. Focus on the speed of your discourse, guaranteeing it lines up with the substance and permits your crowd to successfully ingest the data.

6. **Mirror and Match:**

Reflecting and matching allude to quietly copying the non-verbal communication of the individual you are associating with. This non-verbal procedure constructs compatibility and makes a feeling of association. Focus on the other individual's stance, motions, and speed, and change your own non-verbal prompts in like manner. In any case, practice wariness to try not to seem deceitful or excessively imitative.

7. **Be Aware of Proxemics:**

Proxemics alludes to the utilization of individual space in correspondence. Regard social and individual inclinations with respect to individual space, changing your closeness in like manner. Attacking somebody's very own space can be seen as nosy, while keeping suitable separation cultivates solace and regard. Be receptive to non-verbal prompts flagging solace or inconvenience with nearness.

8. **Utilize Intentional Developments:**

Deliberate developments convey aim and certainty. Abstain from squirming, as it very well may be diverting and subvert your validity. All things considered, utilize purposeful developments to accentuate central issues or to draw in your crowd.

Intentional motions and developments upgrade your generally speaking non-verbal correspondence, making a more cleaned and effective presence.

9. **Exhibit Undivided attention:**

Non-verbal correspondence is a critical part of undivided attention. Exhibit commitment by gesturing in understanding, keeping in touch, and giving non-verbal prompts that signal mindfulness. Keep away from interruptions, for example, actually taking a look at your telephone or glancing around, as these ways of behaving convey lack of engagement. Undivided attention through non-verbal signals cultivates better comprehension and association in discussions.

10. **Focus on Microexpressions:**

Microexpressions are temporary looks that uncover certified feelings. While they happen automatically, monitoring them can give important bits of knowledge into others' sentiments and responses. Train yourself to perceive microexpressions, as they can offer signals about implicit feelings or worries in relational communications.

11. **Control Apprehensive Propensities:**

Apprehensive propensities, like tapping your foot or playing with your hair, can bring down compelling non-verbal correspondence. Recognize and deal with controlling any apprehensive propensities that might be diverting or convey nervousness. Staying cool headed and limiting anxious ways of behaving add to a more sure and created non-verbal presence.

12. **Dress Suitably:**

While not an immediate type of non-verbal communication, your decision of dress and prepping adds to the general impression you convey. Dress properly for the specific situation and crowd, thinking about social standards and assumptions. A very much prepared appearance upgrades your validity and adds to a positive non-verbal picture.

13. **Embrace Reflecting Inspiration:**

Reflecting can stretch out past actual developments to reflect positive feelings and energy. To make a positive and energetic climate, ooze energy through your own non-verbal prompts. Grin, keep an open stance, and express excitement in your motions. Reflecting inspiration can add to an additional elevating and cooperative correspondence climate.

14. **Use Contact Suitably:**

Contact can be a strong type of non-verbal correspondence, however it should be involved sensibly and with thought for social and individual limits. Proper contacts, like a handshake or a congratulatory gesture, can convey warmth and association. In any case, forever be aware of the unique situation and the other individual's solace level with actual contact.

15. **Adjust to Social Contrasts:**

Social standards essentially impact non-verbal correspondence. Various societies might have fluctuating assumptions about eye to eye connection, motions, and individual space. Be delicate to social contrasts, and adjust your non-verbal signs to line up with the social setting. This mindfulness cultivates multifaceted comprehension and powerful correspondence.

16. **Pass Certainty on through Handshake:**

A firm and sure handshake is an exemplary non-verbal prompt that conveys incredible skill and confidence. Practice your handshake to guarantee it is neither too limp nor excessively solid. While starting a handshake, keep in touch and deal a certifiable grin. A sure handshake establishes an uplifting vibe for the cooperation.

17. **Know about Non-Verbal Spillage:**

Non-verbal spillage happens when genuine feelings or aims accidentally surface through non-verbal signs. Know about any incongruence between your verbal and non-verbal messages. For example, on the off chance that you're examining a positive subject however your looks convey distress, it might prompt disarray or question. Take a stab at arrangement between your verbal and non-verbal correspondence to upgrade validness.

18. **Use Vital Stops:**

Quietness and stops are non-verbal components that can add accentuation and effect on your correspondence. Key stops permit audience members to ingest data, underline central issues, and make a feeling of expectation. Stay away from the inclination to fill each second with words, and use stops decisively to upgrade the general cadence and adequacy of your correspondence.

19. **Be Aware of Your Microgestures:**

Microgestures are unobtrusive, fast developments that can convey stowed away feelings or considerations. These can incorporate developments of the hands, looks, or changes in non-verbal communication. While they might slip through the cracks by a lot of people, monitoring your own microgestures and those of others can give significant bits of knowledge into the fundamental elements of a discussion.

20. **Keep up with Consistency:**

Consistency in non-verbal correspondence is fundamental for building trust and believability. Guarantee that your non-verbal communication lines up with your verbal messages. Irregularities between what is said and the way things are communicated non-verbally can make disarray and subvert your general correspondence. Take a stab at congruity and soundness in both verbal and non-verbal components.

21. **Practice Careful Relaxing:**

Careful breathing is a strategy that can assist with managing your sensory system and advance a completely relaxed disposition. Prior to participating in a talking circumstance, take a couple of seconds to rehearse profound, careful relaxing. This basic yet powerful practice can assist with lessening nervousness, further develop center, and add to a general feeling of groundedness.

22. **Look for Criticism and Self-Reflection:**

Routinely look for criticism on your non-verbal correspondence from confided in partners, tutors, or companions. Useful input can give important bits of knowledge into regions to progress. Furthermore, participate in self-reflection by recording your introductions or collaborations and examining your non-verbal signs. This mindfulness adds to progressing refinement and upgrade of your non-verbal relational abilities.

23. **Improve Non-Verbal Correspondence in Virtual Settings:**

As virtual correspondence turns out to be progressively pervasive, adjusting non-verbal signs to online stages is urgent. Keep in touch by gazing straight into the camera, utilize looks to convey feelings, and be aware of your experience and in general appearance. Use motions inside the edge of the camera to upgrade commitment in virtual connections.

24. **Become the best at Non-Verbal Tuning in:**

Listening is a functioning cycle that stretches out past verbal affirmation. Non-verbal listening signs, for example, gesturing, keeping in touch, and reflecting the speaker's feelings, exhibit mindful commitment. Conveying non-verbal signs of undivided attention encourages viable correspondence and fortifies relational associations.

25. **Foster Capacity to understand people on a profound level:**

The ability to appreciate people at their core includes perceiving and grasping feelings, both in oneself as well as other people. Develop the capacity to understand people on a profound level to upgrade your capacity to precisely decipher non-verbal prompts. Being receptive to the feelings communicated through non-verbal communication takes into consideration more compassionate and successful correspondence.

26. **Be Veritable and Legitimate:**

Credibility is a foundation of significant non-verbal correspondence. Be consistent with yourself and express certifiable feelings and aims. Genuineness fabricates trust and impacts others, adding to a more significant and effective association. Keep away from created or misrepresented non-verbal signals, as they can be seen as devious.

27. **Underline Positive Non-Verbal Support:**

Build up certain ways of behaving and achievements through non-verbal prompts. A gesture of congratulations, a thumbs-up signal, or a grin can convey support and acknowledgment. Positive non-verbal support improves inspiration and cultivates a positive and steady correspondence climate.

28. **Adjust Your Non-Verbal Correspondence to Setting:**

Various settings might require changing non-verbal correspondence draws near. Adjust your non-verbal communication, signals, and articulations in view of the custom of the setting, the idea of the discussion, and the social setting. Being versatile in your non-verbal correspondence guarantees that you can actually explore assorted social and expert situations.

29. **Foster Non-Verbal Mindfulness in Social environments:**

In social scenes, non-verbal mindfulness turns out to be especially significant. Focus on the elements of the gathering, and utilize your non-verbal communication to draw in with various people. Appropriate eye to eye connection, differ your motions, and be aware of the general energy of the gathering. Compelling non-verbal correspondence in social environments adds to a firm and cooperative climate.

30. **Observe Non-Verbal Variety:**

Non-verbal correspondence styles can fluctuate broadly among people and societies. Commend this variety and be available to grasping different non-verbal prompts. Perceive that signals, articulations, and non-verbal communication might convey exceptional implications across different foundations. Move toward non-verbal variety with interest and regard.

5.3 Capturing attention from the start and maintaining engagement

Catching and keeping up with consideration is a principal challenge in different parts of correspondence, whether it's public talking, composing, educating, or introducing. In a world immersed with data and interruptions, the capacity to catch a crowd of people's eye all along and support their commitment is an important expertise. This far reaching investigation dives into methodologies and procedures to charm consideration and keep crowds locked in.

1. **Begin with a Convincing Snare:**

   The initial snapshots of any correspondence piece are basic. Start with a convincing snare that gets consideration and provokes interest. This can be an intriguing inquiry, an astounding reality, a convincing story, or a strong assertion. A solid opening establishes the vibe for commitment and captivates the crowd to put their consideration in what follows.

2. **Understand Your Listeners' perspective:**

   Understanding your crowd is central to catching and keeping up with their consideration. Tailor your substance to reverberate with their inclinations, inclinations, and necessities. Think about their socio-economics, foundation, and assumptions. A crowd of people driven approach guarantees that your correspondence is pertinent and con-vincing to those you are tending to.

3. **Make a Reasonable and Succinct Message:**

   Clearness is critical to keeping up with crowd consideration. Create an unmistakable and brief message that conveys your central matters really. Stay away from pointless language or intricacy that could befuddle your crowd. A clear and effectively edible message upgrades cognizance and keeps audience members locked in.

4. **Use Visuals Decisively:**

   Visual components are strong consideration grabbers. Consolidate con-vincing visuals like pictures, diagrams, graphs, or slides to supplement your message. Visuals upgrade understanding as well as change up the show, forestalling repetitiveness. Guarantee that visuals are pertinent, excellent, and support the central issues you need to convey.

5. **Integrate Narrating Strategies:**

   People are wired to answer stories. Incorporate narrating strategies into your correspondence to make a story that enraptures your crowd. Indi-vidual accounts, contextual investigations, or fictitious situations can add a close to home and interesting aspect to your message. Stories make an association and support interest all through your correspondence.

6. **Fluctuate Your Tone and Speed:**

   Tedium can rapidly prompt withdrawal. Shift your manner of speaking and speed to keep up with interest. Use accentuation, stops, and tweak to feature central issues and make a unique cadence. A very much paced conveyance keeps the crowd mindful and adds a layer of expressiveness to your correspondence.

7. **Encourage Intuitiveness:**

Energize crowd investment and collaboration to keep them locked in. Offer conversation starters, work with conversations, or integrate intelligent components like surveys or back and forth discussions. Dynamic support changes the correspondence into a two-way discourse, causing the crowd to feel included and put resources into the substance.

8. **Use Humor Suitably:**

Humor is a powerful instrument for catching consideration and encouraging a positive environment. Suitably coordinated and applicable humor can loosen things up, ease strain, and make your correspondence more pleasant. Be aware of the unique situation and the sensibilities of your crowd, guaranteeing that humor lines up with the general tone and reason for your message.

9. **Address the WIIFM (How might this benefit Me):**

Crowds are bound to stay drew in when they see individual pertinence in the substance. Obviously expressive the advantages or worth that your message offers to the crowd. Answer the inquiry, "How might this benefit me?" to exhibit the commonsense meaning of the data you are sharing.

10. **Lay out Believability:**

Building believability is fundamental for keeping up with crowd consideration. Lay out your mastery and dependability from the get-go in your correspondence. Share pertinent qualifications, encounters, or information that show your insight regarding the matter. A solid speaker or communicator is bound to hold the crowd's consideration.

11. **Utilize Logical Gadgets:**

Logical gadgets add style and influence to your correspondence. Utilize procedures like redundancy, similar sounding word usage, or non-serious inquiries to make an important and drawing in experience. Very much positioned logical gadgets improve the musicality and effect of your message, making it more convincing for the crowd.

12. **Influence the Force of Shock:**

Amazing your crowd with startling turns, experiences, or disclosures can shock them out of lack of concern and reignite their advantage. Whether it's an amazing measurement, a strange finding, or an unforeseen turn in your story, snapshots of shock catch consideration and make your correspondence essential.

13. **Show Energy and Excitement:**

Energy is infectious. Express authentic energy for your theme to charm your crowd. Allow your energy to radiate through your voice, looks, and non-verbal communication. An excited speaker conveys energy and conviction, making a positive and drawing in air.

14. **Separate Complex Ideas:**

Assuming that your message includes complex ideas, separate them into absorbable pieces. Use relationships, illustrations, or certifiable guides to work on mind boggling thoughts. Making data open and reasonable guarantees that your crowd stays connected as opposed to feeling overpowered by intricacy.

15. **Use Multi-Tactile Allure:**

Appeal to various faculties to improve commitment. Consolidate visuals for sight, use stories that summon feelings, and consider integrating pertinent sounds or music. A multi-tangible methodology makes a more extravagant and more vivid experience for the crowd, making your correspondence more important.

16. **Address Trouble spots and Arrangements:**

Recognize and address the trouble spots or difficulties your crowd might confront. Obviously eloquent how your message gives arrangements or addresses their interests. Showing that you get it and identify with their necessities keeps up with importance and keeps the crowd put resources into tracking down arrangements through your correspondence.

17. **Fabricate a Convincing Story Curve:**

Structure your correspondence with a story circular segment that incorporates a reasonable start, center, and end. Present the contention or challenge, construct pressure, and resolve it with a wonderful end. A very much built account curve supports revenue and guides the crowd through a durable and convincing story.

18. **Be Aware of Timing:**

Successful timing is pivotal for keeping up with commitment. Be aware of the general span of your correspondence, as well as the pacing of individual segments. Try not to over-burden your crowd with data or delaying without clear movement. Regard your crowd's time and consideration by conveying content that is succinct and very much paced.

19. **Appeal to Feelings:**

Feelings assume a huge part in catching and holding consideration. Appeal to your crowd's feelings by consolidating components that summon compassion, satisfaction, interest, or even a need to keep moving. Close to home reverberation makes a more profound association and improves the general effect of your correspondence.

20. **Cultivate an Engaging Persona:**

    An interesting and true persona makes you more receptive to your crowd. Share individual stories, encounters, or difficulties that acculturate you. An engaging speaker is bound to lay out a veritable association with the crowd, encouraging trust and supporting their advantage.

21. **Consolidate Shock Components:**

    Acquaint shock components decisively with upset consistency and reconnect the crowd. This could include startling visuals, changes in tone, or intelligent components that blow some minds. Shocks revive interest and interest, keeping the crowd from blocking out because of consistency.

22. **Measure and Answer Crowd Input:**

    Effectively measure crowd responses and change your methodology in light of their criticism. Focus on non-verbal signs, like looks and non-verbal communication, to evaluate commitment levels. On the off chance that you sense a plunge in consideration, be ready to adjust your substance or conveyance to reconnect your crowd.

23. **Underline the Significance of the Data:**

    Obviously convey why the data you're sharing is significant or important. Laying out the meaning of your message inspires the crowd to remain mindful. Whether it's taking care of an issue, quickly jumping all over a chance, or acquiring significant experiences, stressing the significance makes a feeling of direction for the crowd.

24. **Use Innovation Imaginatively:**

    Consolidate innovation imaginatively to upgrade commitment. This could incorporate intuitive introductions, mixed media components, or computer generated reality encounters. Influence innovation to establish a dynamic and vivid climate that lines up with the substance of your message.

25. **Carry out the "Interest Hole":**

    Make an oddity hole by introducing an inquiry, situation, or mystery that leaves the crowd needing to know more. This procedure supports dynamic commitment as audience members expect the goal of the interest hole. The craving for conclusion supports consideration all through your correspondence.

26. **Give Open doors to Reflection:**

    Consolidate snapshots of reflection inside your correspondence. Interruption to permit the crowd to retain data, think about central issues, or offer their considerations. Reflection spans give breathing space and improve by and large commitment by empowering dynamic mental handling.

27. **Adjust to Various Learning Styles:**

Individuals have different learning styles, including visual, hear-able, and sensation inclinations. Adjust your correspondence to take care of various learning styles. Use a blend of visuals, expressed clarifications, and intuitive components to oblige an expansive scope of inclinations, upgrading in general commitment.

28. **Exhibit Openness and Inclusivity:**

Establish a comprehensive climate by guaranteeing that your correspondence is open to a different crowd. Utilize comprehensive language, give elective organizations to visual substance, and think about assorted points of view. A comprehensive methodology encourages a feeling of having a place and keeps all crowd individuals locked in.

29. **Explore different avenues regarding Eccentric Methodologies:**

At times, split away from traditional ways to deal with catch consideration. Try different things with capricious components, like astonishment visitors, unpredictable visuals, or intelligent exercises. Unconventionality flashes interest and keeps your crowd inquisitive about what will occur straightaway.

30. **End with Effect:**

Similarly as the start is essential, the end is as well. End your correspondence with influence, having an enduring impression. Sum up central issues, re-underline your fundamental message, or finish up with a source of inspiration. A solid end guarantees that the crowd leaves with a reasonable important point and a feeling of satisfaction.

5.4 Q&A strategies and handling unexpected challenges

Q & A (back and forth) discussions are vital parts of different expert and public cooperations, going from introductions and talks to board conversations and meetings. Successfully overseeing back and forth discussions requires a mix of readiness, versatility, and relational abilities. This exhaustive investigation digs into techniques for taking care of interactive discussions and exploring surprising difficulties that might emerge.

1. **Expect and Get ready:**

Readiness is vital to effectively exploring interactive discussions. Expect possible inquiries by thinking about the points of view and worries of your crowd. Survey your substance and recognize regions that might produce requests. Get ready smart and brief reactions to normal inquiries, guaranteeing that you are exceptional to address a scope of subjects.

2. **Set Clear Rules:**

Lay out clear rules for the interactive discussion toward the start of your show or conversation. Impart the arrangement, time requirements, and a particular points you are available to tending to. Urge members to pose inquiries connected with the show content and guide them on the favored way of asking (e.g., lifting hands, utilizing a receiver). Clear rules set assumptions and establish an organized climate for back and forth discussion.

3. **Make a Positive Air:**

Encourage a positive and open climate for the interactive discussion. Urge members to share their considerations and inquiries unafraid of judgment. Express appreciation for questions and accentuate the worth of different points of view. Establishing an inviting climate supports crowd commitment and improves the probability of significant connections during the back and forth discussion.

4. **Rehash or Explain Questions:**

After an inquiry is presented, rehash or explain it to guarantee everybody in the crowd heard and comprehended. Rewording the inquiry likewise gives you a second to process and figure out a reasonable reaction. This training is especially significant in huge or assembly room style settings where crowd individuals might be situated a long way from the individual posing the inquiry.

5. **Be Compact and Direct:**

While answering inquiries, make progress toward clearness and brevity. Stay away from extended or wandering responses that might weaken your message. Conveying compact reactions regards the crowd's time and keeps the back and forth discussion centered. In the event that extra setting is required, propose to give more subtleties after the meeting or throughout a break.

6. **Recognize Legitimacy of Inquiries:**

Recognize the legitimacy of each inquiry, regardless of whether it challenges your perspective. Communicating appreciation for different points of view encourages a deferential and open discourse. On the off chance that an inquiry is hazy or requires explanation, look for explanation from the examiner to guarantee you address their interests precisely.

7. **Oversee Time Successfully:**

Designate a particular measure of time for the interactive discussion and oversee it reasonably. Assuming time imperatives are tight, focus on questions that are extensively important or agent of normal worries. Assuming an inside and out conversation is justified, think about booking extra time or proposing to proceed with the discussion outside the conventional meeting.

8. **Keep cool-headed and Created:**

Keep a completely relaxed disposition, even despite testing or unforeseen inquiries. In the event that an inquiry surprises you, pause for a minute to accumulate your contemplations prior to answering. Try not to become protective, and on second thought, move toward each inquiry with a useful and formed demeanor.

9. **Make sure to Say "I Don't Have any idea":**

It's completely OK to recognize when you don't have a response to a specific inquiry. On the off chance that you experience an inquiry outside your skill or on a point you haven't completely investigated, speak the truth about it. Express a readiness to investigate the matter further or propose to interface the examiner with somebody who might have more data.

10. **Divert When Vital:**

In the event that an inquiry is outside the extent of your show or not lined up with the expected concentration, carefully divert the conversation. Recognize the inquiry and make sense of that while it could be a significant point, the ongoing meeting is centered around a particular topic. Propose to resolve the inquiry later or recommend elective roads for acquiring the data looked for.

11. **Empower Crowd Support:**

Effectively empower crowd support by welcoming inquiries according to different viewpoints. Draw in with various segments of the crowd to guarantee a different scope of inquiries. In the event that the crowd is reluctant to seek clarification on pressing issues, consider consolidating intelligent components, for example, surveys or little gathering conversations to animate support.

12. **Extension to Key Messages:**

Utilize the interactive discussion as a chance to support key messages from your show. While answering inquiries, span back to the primary subjects or important points you believe the crowd should keep in mind. This supports your focal message and guarantees that in any event, testing questions add to the general rationality of your correspondence.

13. **Be Aware of Non-Verbal Prompts:**

Focus on non-verbal prompts from the two examiners and the more extensive crowd. Looks, non-verbal communication, and crowd responses can give significant bits of knowledge into the effect of your reactions. Be sensitive to these signals to measure the crowd's commitment and change your methodology likewise.

14. **Oversee Crowd Elements:**

In circumstances where various crowd individuals are anxious to pose inquiries all the while, deal with the elements by laying out an unmistakable cycle. This might include utilizing a lifted hand framework, dispersing mouthpieces, or utilizing a computerized stage for submitting questions. Successfully overseeing crowd elements guarantees a fair and coordinated back and forth discussion.

15. **Consider Board Approaches:**

In board conversations, coordinate with individual specialists to guarantee a strong and cooperative back and forth discussion experience. Settle on a procedure for sharing the chance to answer questions and stay away from overt repetitiveness. In the event that specialists hold assorted points of view, influence this variety to give extensive and nuanced replies.

16. **Be Available to Helpful Analysis:**

Embrace helpful analysis with a receptive outlook. In the event that an inquiry contains components of study or difficulties your point of view, view it as a chance for development. Answer thoughtfully, recognize contrasting perspectives, and, if material, share your reasoning or extra setting. An eagerness to draw in with helpful analysis improves your believability and shows receptiveness.

17. **Give Noteworthy Focus points:**

While resolving questions, endeavor to give noteworthy focus points or functional experiences. Consider how your reactions can add to the crowd's comprehension or illuminate their navigation. Unmistakable and pertinent data increases the value of the back and forth discussion and improves the crowd's general insight.

18. **Look for Explanation for Uncertain Inquiries:**

In the event that an inquiry is vague or hazy, look for explanation from the examiner. Rework the inquiry to affirm your comprehension and guarantee that your reaction tends to the expected request. Explaining equivocal inquiries encourages better correspondence and forestalls false impressions.

19. **Handle Threatening Inquiries Nimbly:**

Infrequently, speakers might experience threatening or fierce inquiries. Handle such inquiries nimbly by keeping a cool head and ceasing from answering in a fierce way. Address the fundamental worries brought up by the issue as opposed to taking part in a cautious trade. Divert the concentration to valuable discourse.

20. **Assess and Repeat:**

After the back and forth discussion, carve out opportunity to think about the experience. Assess the sorts of inquiries represented, the adequacy of your reactions, and any regions for development. Utilize this input to emphasize and refine your question and answer systems for future commitment. Ceaseless reflection adds to continuous development as a communicator.

21. **Embrace Innovation for Virtual question and answer session:**

   In virtual settings, influence innovation to improve the question and answer session experience. Use computerized stages that permit members to submit inquiries progressively or through an assigned channel. Consider consolidating live talk highlights, virtual surveys, or intelligent components to work with commitment in virtual back and forth discussions.

22. **Give Assets to Additional Investigation:**

   In the event that an inquiry requires more top to bottom investigation or on the other hand assuming the crowd communicates revenue in extra assets, be ready to give follow-up materials. This could incorporate references, articles, or connections to important substance. Offering assets for additional investigation exhibits your obligation to supporting continuous learning.

23. **Cultivate Inclusivity and Different Voices:**

   Advance inclusivity by effectively looking for inquiries from people with different viewpoints. Energize members from different foundations to share their bits of knowledge and requests. Cultivating a different scope of voices adds to a more extravagant and more thorough interactive discussion.

24. **Adjust to Startling Specialized Issues:**

   In virtual or innovation subordinate back and forth discussions, be ready to adjust to unforeseen specialized difficulties. Have emergency courses of action set up, for example, elective correspondence channels or reinforcement gadgets. Stay cool headed to explore unanticipated specialized issues without disturbing the progression of the back and forth discussion.

25. **Address Delicate Subjects with Responsiveness:**

   On the off chance that questions address touchy or disputable subjects, address them with awareness and mindfulness. Recognize the intricacy of the issue, give setting, and express a readiness to participate in a deferential exchange. Showing sympathy and regard in addressing delicate subjects adds to a useful question and answer climate.

26. **Energize Follow-Up Correspondence:**

   In circumstances where time requirements limit the profundity of question and answer conversations, empower follow-up correspondence. Welcome members to connect by means of email, virtual entertainment, or assigned correspondence channels for additional conversations or explanations. This approach broadens the chance for proceeded with commitment past the proper meeting.

27. **Lay out Limits:**

While empowering support, it's fundamental to lay out limits to guarantee an engaged and conscious question and answer climate. Obviously impart rules for fitting way of behaving and question content. Address any problematic way of behaving quickly and carefully to keep a useful environment.

28. **Be Aware of Social Responsive qualities:**

In assorted and multicultural settings, be aware of social responsive qualities while resolving questions. Perceive that correspondence styles, assumptions, and no points might differ across societies. Move toward inquiries with social responsiveness, and be available to adjusting your correspondence style to line up with assorted social standards.

29. **Practice Undivided attention:**

Undivided attention is urgent during back and forth discussions. Give close consideration to each question, guaranteeing that you completely handle the subtleties and aims behind the requests. Practice intelligent tuning in by summarizing questions and affirming understanding prior to answering. Undivided attention improves the nature of your reactions and cultivates a more profound association with the crowd.

30. **Offer Thanks:**

Finish up the interactive discussion by offering thanks to the crowd for their support and insightful inquiries. Recognize the worth of their commitments and the improving discourse that occurred. Offering thanks makes a positive and grateful tone, having an enduring impact on the crowd.

Chapter 6

Leveraging Technology and Multimedia

Utilizing innovation and interactive media has turned into a fundamental part of our contemporary presence, changing the manner in which we convey, learn, work, and engage ourselves. In this period of fast mechanical headway, the coordination of assorted media components has upgraded our encounters as well as altered different ventures.

One of the essential spaces significantly affected by the combination of innovation and interactive media is training. Conventional strategies for instructing and learning have gone through a significant transformation, with the coming of intuitive mixed media devices and computerized assets. Instructive establishments overall have embraced the force of innovation to establish drawing in and vivid learning conditions.

Computerized course readings, intuitive reenactments, and instructive applications have supplanted traditional pieces of literature, furnishing understudies with a dynamic and intelligent opportunity for growth. The mix of sight and sound components, like recordings, movements, and reenactments, empowers understudies to actually embrace complex ideas more. Visual and hear-able guides improve the maintenance of data, taking care of different learning styles and cultivating a more profound comprehension of subjects.

Moreover, e-learning stages and monstrous open internet based courses (MOOCs) have democratized schooling by making learning open to a worldwide crowd. Students can get to top notch instructive substance from famous foundations and specialists, separating geological obstructions and advancing long lasting learning.

In the domain of medical care, innovation and sight and sound play had a critical impact in clinical schooling, patient consideration, and examination. Computer generated reality (VR) and increased reality (AR) have been used to mimic surgeries, furnishing clinical understudies with a sensible and sans risk climate to rehearse and refine their abilities. This not just improves the skill of future medical services experts yet additionally adds to patient wellbeing.

Besides, mixed media advancements have changed patient schooling by working on complex clinical data. Intuitive recordings, livelinesss, and virtual visits can explain ailments, treatment methods, and preventive measures, engaging patients to come to informed conclusions about their wellbeing.

In the business scene, innovation and mixed media have reformed correspondence and coordinated effort. Virtual gatherings, online classes, and video meetings have become fundamental apparatuses for distant cooperation, empowering groups to associate and work consistently across geological limits. The combination of sight and sound components in introductions and correspondence materials improves lucidity and commitment, making data more available and convincing.

The ascent of online entertainment stages has additionally enhanced the effect of mixed media in business. Organizations influence media content, including recordings, infographics, and intelligent posts, to associate with their main interest group, construct brand mindfulness, and drive client commitment. The visual and intelligent nature of interactive media content works with successful narrating and brand correspondence.

In the field of showcasing, sight and sound assumes a focal part in making convincing and essential missions. Video commercials, intuitive sites, and vivid encounters have become standard devices for advertisers to catch the consideration of shoppers in a jam-packed computerized scene. Expanded reality applications permit clients to imagine items in their own current circumstance prior to making a buy, improving the web based shopping experience.

Diversion, an industry intrinsically attached to mixed media, has gone through a change in outlook with progressions in innovation. Web-based features, internet gaming, computer generated reality encounters, and intelligent narrating have reshaped how we consume and draw in with amusement content. The combination of innovation and mixed media has democratized content creation, permitting autonomous makers to contact worldwide crowds through stages like YouTube, TikTok, and podcasting.

The gaming business, specifically, has seen a groundbreaking contact with the combination of state of the art innovations. Top notch illustrations, sensible reproductions, and vivid narrating have raised gaming encounters higher than ever. Computer generated reality gaming gives players a feeling of presence and cooperation, obscuring the lines between the virtual and genuine universes.

The impact of innovation and mixed media is likewise apparent in the manner news and data are spread. Computerized reporting has turned into the standard, with online stages, digital broadcasts, and web-based entertainment filling in as essential wellsprings of information for some people. Mixed media components, like recordings, infographics, and intelligent outlines, upgrade the narrating capacities of columnists and give crowds a more extravagant comprehension of information occasions.

In any case, the fast spread of data through advanced channels additionally presents difficulties connected with falsehood and the requirement for media proficiency. The straightforwardness with which mixed media content can be controlled raises worries about the validness and dependability of online data. Subsequently, there is a developing accentuation on media proficiency schooling to engage people to assess and explore the computerized scene basically.

The domain of workmanship and imagination has encountered a renaissance with the incorporation of innovation and sight and sound. Computerized workmanship, virtual shows, and intelligent establishments have extended the opportunities for imaginative articulation. Specialists influence interactive media instruments to make vivid encounters that connect with the faculties and summon close to home reactions from crowds.

Innovation has likewise democratized the inventive strategy, empowering people to investigate their creative tendencies through computerized instruments. Stages that give admittance to stock photographs, music, and plan components enable makers to rejuvenate their thoughts without the requirement for broad assets. The web fills in as an immense material for sharing and displaying different types of imaginative articulation.

As innovation keeps on propelling, the Web of Things (IoT) has arisen as a key empowering influence of network and mechanization. Ordinary items are outfitted with sensors and availability, making an organization of interconnected gadgets. This interconnectedness considers the consistent trade of information, prompting upgraded effectiveness and accommodation in different parts of life.

Savvy homes, furnished with IoT gadgets, offer inhabitants command over different capabilities, including lighting, security, and environment control, through incorporated sight and sound points of interaction. Wearable gadgets, for example, smartwatches and wellness trackers, influence mixed media components to convey data and notices in an easy to use way. The coordination of IoT in medical services gadgets empowers remote observing and customized wellbeing experiences.

The appearance of computerized reasoning (artificial intelligence) has additionally sped up the mix of innovation and media. Simulated intelligence driven calculations investigate huge datasets to customize client encounters, suggest content, and anticipate inclinations. Menial helpers, fueled by computer based intelligence, use normal language handling and media points of interaction to furnish clients with data and perform errands through voice orders.

In the domain of independent vehicles, media interfaces assume a urgent part in improving the driver and traveler experience. Infotainment frameworks, increased reality shows, and voice acknowledgment innovations add to a more secure and more pleasant driving experience. The combination of computer based intelligence empowers vehicles to decipher and answer media inputs, adding to the improvement of self-driving vehicles.

Be that as it may, the broad reception of innovation and interactive media raises moral contemplations connected with protection, security, and the potential for unseen side-effects. The assortment and use of individual information for designated promoting, the gamble of digital assaults on associated gadgets, and the moral ramifications of artificial intelligence independent direction are subjects of continuous discussion and investigation.

The crossing point of innovation and interactive media additionally holds huge ramifications for the eventual fate of work. Computerization, filled by progressions in artificial intelligence and mechanical technology, is changing enterprises and reshaping the idea of occupations. While robotization can possibly build effectiveness and efficiency, it likewise raises worries about work dislodging and the requirement for upskilling and reskilling.

Remote work, worked with by innovation and mixed media specialized devices, has turned into a pervasive pattern, offering adaptability and openness to representatives. Notwithstanding, it likewise presents difficulties connected with balance between fun and serious activities, advanced exhaustion, and the disintegration of customary work environment limits. As the idea of work advances, there is a developing accentuation on fostering a computerized smart labor force furnished with the abilities important for the advanced age.

The combination of innovation and sight and sound in metropolitan preparation and design has prompted the improvement of shrewd urban communities. These urban communities influence interconnected advancements to upgrade productivity, supportability, and the general personal satisfaction for occupants. Sight and sound points of interaction openly spaces, intelligent metropolitan shows, and increased reality applications add to a seriously captivating and associated metropolitan climate.

Ecological manageability is a squeezing worldwide concern, and innovation assumes a double part in both adding to natural difficulties and offering arrangements. The assembling and removal of electronic gadgets add to electronic waste, while the energy utilization of advanced framework presents natural effects. On the other side, innovation likewise empowers advancements in sustainable power, natural observing, and reasonable practices.

6.1 Incorporating visuals and multimedia for enhanced impact

Consolidating visuals and sight and sound has turned into a key system across different areas to enhance influence, impart really, and connect with crowds in an undeniably computerized and outwardly determined world. The combination of pictures, recordings, infographics, and intuitive components has risen above conventional correspondence hindrances, making a more vivid and convincing experience for people in training, business, showcasing, reporting, and then some.

In the domain of training, the coordination of visuals and media has altered the learning scene. Conventional course books and talks are giving way to dynamic computerized content that use the force of visuals to improve understanding and maintenance. Instructive recordings, intelligent reenactments, and computer generated reality encounters have become significant devices in homerooms, taking special care of different learning styles and cultivating a seriously captivating instructive climate.

The viability of visuals in training is established in the mental rule that people cycle and recall data all the more proficiently when introduced in a visual configuration. Complex ideas can be rearranged through infographics, outlines, and charts, giving understudies visual guides that supplement text based data. Additionally, mixed media components, for example, activitys and reenactments, rejuvenate theoretical ideas, making learning more intelligent and pleasant.

E-learning stages and Huge Open Web-based Courses (MOOCs) have profited by the capability of interactive media to democratize instruction, separating geological boundaries and giving admittance to quality learning assets for a worldwide crowd. Video addresses, intelligent tests, and cooperative web-based discussions make a rich and various growth opportunity that reaches out past the bounds of conventional study halls.

In the corporate world, the utilization of visuals and sight and sound has turned into a foundation of compelling correspondence and preparing. Organizations utilize mixed media components in introductions, preparing modules, and interior correspondences to pass on data in an unmistakable, compact, and outwardly engaging way. The combination of visuals helps with the maintenance of basic data and guarantees that representatives stay drew in and informed.

Visual correspondence is especially vital with regards to information and investigation. Infographics and information representations distil complex datasets into available and conceivable configurations, empowering partners to rapidly get a handle on experiences. Dashboards with intuitive visual components engage chiefs to investigate information patterns, recognize examples, and settle on informed decisions, adding to information driven decision-production inside associations.

The utilization of media reaches out to the domain of promoting, where visuals assume a critical part in catching consideration, passing on brand messages, and impacting purchaser conduct. In the advanced age, purchasers are immersed with data, and the ability to focus is temporary. Visual substance, like pictures, recordings, and infographics, has demonstrated to be more successful in getting and holding consideration contrasted with text-just happy.

Virtual entertainment stages have become strong vehicles for visual narrating and brand correspondence. Organizations influence media content to make outwardly convincing accounts that resound with their ideal interest group. Visual stages like Instagram, Pinterest, and TikTok blossom with the sharing and utilization of outwardly engaging substance, giving organizations open doors to exhibit items, share in the background sees, and associate with customers on a more private level.

Video showcasing has arisen as a prevailing power in the computerized promoting scene. Whether through short special recordings, instructive substance, or narrating efforts, recordings can convey feelings, construct brand character, and drive commitment. Live streaming further improves the intelligent viewpoint, permitting organizations to associate with their crowd progressively and get quick criticism.

In the field of reporting, the mix of visuals and media has changed how news is introduced and consumed. Conventional print media has advanced into computerized stages where articles are improved with pictures, recordings, and intelligent components. Media narrating permits writers to convey the profundity and setting of a story, drenching the crowd in an additional exhaustive and instinctive story.

Intelligent infographics and information representations are utilized to upgrade the comprehension of mind boggling reports. Visual portrayals of information furnish perusers with a more nuanced viewpoint on issues, cultivating a more prominent mindfulness and appreciation for the complexities of the topic. Furthermore, mixed media components empower news associations to adjust to changing buyer inclinations, as crowds progressively look for dynamic and connecting with content.

The domain of workmanship and imagination has encountered a computerized renaissance with the incorporation of interactive media. Computerized workmanship, augmented reality establishments, and intelligent shows rethink the limits of imaginative articulation. Specialists influence innovation to make vivid encounters that draw in numerous faculties, welcoming crowds to partake in the innovative approach and obscure the lines among onlooker and maker.

Computerized stages and online entertainment act as worldwide displays, permitting craftsmen to exhibit their work to a tremendous and various crowd. The democratization of craftsmanship through advanced apparatuses empowers arising specialists to earn perceivability and respect without the conventional watchmen.

Also, interactive media craftsmanship challenges customary ideas of medium and structure, pushing the limits of inventiveness and welcoming new viewpoints.

Innovation has not just impacted the creation and utilization of craftsmanship however has likewise turned into a mechanism for imaginative articulation itself. Sight and sound establishments, intelligent exhibitions, and augmented reality encounters submerge crowds in novel and provocative creative undertakings. This convergence of innovation and workmanship extends the opportunities for inventive articulation as well as mirrors the advancing connection among humankind and innovation.

The fuse of visuals and interactive media isn't restricted to the domain of diversion however has likewise pervaded the areas of science and exploration. Logical correspondence has advanced past scholarly papers and gatherings, with analysts using interactive media to convey their discoveries to more extensive crowds. Infographics, recordings, and intuitive introductions make complex logical ideas open to non-subject matter experts, encouraging public comprehension of logical progressions.

In the field of medication, visuals and media assume essential part in schooling, patient correspondence, and exploration. Clinical imaging advances, for example, X-ray and CT checks, create visual information that guides in analysis and treatment arranging. Instructive recordings and intuitive reproductions assist clinical experts with improving their abilities and keep up to date with the most recent headways in medical care.

Patient schooling has been changed by sight and sound devices, empowering medical care suppliers to pass on clinical data in a conceivable and connecting with way. Intuitive movements, virtual voyages through methods, and sight and sound aides engage patients to come to informed conclusions about their wellbeing. This works on understanding results as well as encourages a cooperative and informed medical care climate.

As innovation keeps on propelling, the mix of computerized reasoning (simulated intelligence) and expanded reality (AR) further upgrades the effect of visuals and interactive media. Artificial intelligence calculations investigate client inclinations to suggest customized content, making mixed media encounters more custom-made and pertinent. AR overlays advanced data onto this present reality, offering clients an improved and intelligent perspective on their environmental elements.

The Web of Things (IoT) expands the venture of media into the texture of daily existence. Brilliant gadgets with media interfaces change homes, urban communities, and working environments into interconnected biological systems.

Voice-enacted colleagues, shrewd mirrors, and increased reality applications make a consistent incorporation of innovation and mixed media, improving everyday encounters and furnishing clients with better approaches to collaborate with their surroundings.

Notwithstanding, the far and wide reception of visuals and mixed media additionally raises moral contemplations, especially with regards to deepfakes and controlled content. The straightforwardness with which interactive media can be adjusted postures difficulties to the realness and reliability of visual data. Subsequently, there is a developing requirement for computerized education and decisive reasoning abilities to explore the complicated scene of visual media and perceive among certifiable and controlled content.

6.2 Utilizing technology to reach wider audiences

Using innovation to contact more extensive crowds has turned into a central technique across different spaces, changing how data is scattered, items are promoted, and benefits are conveyed. In a time where network and digitalization are universal, utilizing innovation isn't just a need yet additionally a vital driver for progress in schooling, business, diversion, medical care, and then some.

Schooling has seen a significant change in reach and openness because of the mix of innovation. Internet learning stages, online courses, and instructive applications have democratized training, empowering people from assorted foundations and geological areas to get to great learning assets. The adaptability presented by innovation permits students to draw in with instructive substance at their own speed, separating conventional boundaries to schooling.

Huge Open Web-based Courses (MOOCs) represent the capability of innovation in contacting a worldwide crowd. These web-based courses, frequently presented by prestigious foundations, take care of students around the world, giving admittance to master drove guidance and assets. Video addresses, intuitive tests, and conversation gatherings make a dynamic and connecting with growth opportunity, encouraging a feeling of local area among students scattered across the globe.

In the corporate scene, innovation fills in as an impetus for contacting more extensive crowds in the domain of business correspondence and showcasing. Virtual gatherings, online courses, and video conferencing devices have become fundamental for far off joint effort, permitting groups to associate flawlessly regardless of geological distances. This improves correspondence inside associations as well as empowers organizations to draw in with clients, accomplices, and partners on a worldwide scale.

Advanced promoting, fueled by innovation, has re-imagined how organizations reach and connect with their interest groups. Virtual entertainment stages, website improvement (Web optimization), and web based promoting empower organizations to expand their arrive at past

nearby business sectors. The capacity to tailor advertising messages in view of client conduct and inclinations improves the adequacy of missions, guaranteeing that content resounds with explicit crowds.

Internet business stages influence innovation to universally arrive at shoppers. Online commercial centers, upheld by secure installment doors and smoothed out operations, work with the deal and conveyance of items to clients all over the planet. Versatile applications give a helpful way to buyers to peruse, shop, and make buys, making items open to a different and extensive crowd.

Media outlets has gone through a change in perspective in reach and dispersion through mechanical headways. Web-based features, video-sharing stages, and computerized content conveyance have changed how amusement is consumed. Crowds can get to a huge range of content, including films, Network programs, music, and gaming, from for all intents and purposes anyplace with a web association.

Web-based entertainment stages have arisen as persuasive devices for content makers to contact more extensive crowds. Stages like YouTube, Instagram, and TikTok permit people to exhibit their gifts, share innovative works, and construct a worldwide following. The viral idea of content on these stages empowers makers to earn perceivability and respect on an exceptional scale.

Live streaming has turned into a famous road for contacting more extensive crowds continuously. Whether through live transmissions via web-based entertainment or devoted streaming stages, people and organizations can associate with crowds around the world, encouraging commitment and intelligence. Virtual occasions, shows, and exhibitions contact crowds past actual imperatives, making vivid encounters for members around the world.

The medical services industry has likewise embraced innovation to grow its compass and work on understanding consideration. Telemedicine, empowered by video conferencing and computerized specialized instruments, permits medical care experts to give distant counsels and clinical exhortation. This is especially significant in arriving at patients in rustic or underserved regions, where admittance to medical care might be restricted.

Versatile wellbeing applications and wearable gadgets engage people to effectively screen their wellbeing and health. These advancements give continuous information, customized bits of knowledge, and remote checking abilities, broadening the range of medical care past conventional clinical settings. Patients can get to wellbeing data, get prescription updates, and take part in virtual counsels, adding to a more understanding driven approach.

The mix of innovation in news and reporting has changed the spread of data, making news open to a worldwide crowd continuously. Online news gateways, versatile applications, and virtual entertainment stages give quick admittance to making it known and refreshes. Mixed media components, for example, recordings and intelligent designs, improve the narrating and commitment parts of information content.

Resident reporting, worked with by innovation, empowers people to report and share news according to their viewpoints. Online entertainment stages act as stages for continuous revealing, permitting situation to unfurl in the public eye. In any case, the fast dispersal of data through these channels likewise raises worries about the precision and dependability of information, underlining the requirement for media education and truth checking.

The use of innovation in logical examination and correspondence has extended the span of logical information. Open-access diaries, online information bases, and cooperative exploration stages empower scientists to impart discoveries to a worldwide crowd. Virtual meetings and online courses interface researchers and specialists around the world, cultivating cooperation and the trading of thoughts.

Innovation plays had an essential impact in emergency correspondence and catastrophe reaction, permitting data to quickly arrive at impacted populaces. Crisis cautions, virtual entertainment refreshes, and online stages disperse basic data during catastrophic events, general wellbeing crises, and different emergencies. The instantaneousness and reach of advanced correspondence add to additional powerful and facilitated reactions.

The job of innovation in language interpretation and restriction has additionally improved worldwide correspondence. Interpretation applications, language-learning stages, and ongoing language interpretation devices separate language obstructions, working with correspondence across assorted semantic foundations. This is especially huge in contacting more extensive crowds in global business, tact, and diverse cooperations.

In the field of horticulture, innovation can possibly arrive at ranchers with imaginative answers for reasonable practices and expanded efficiency. Portable applications furnish ranchers with constant weather conditions conjectures, market costs, and horticultural guidance. Accuracy horticulture innovations, for example, robots and sensors, empower ranchers to improve crop the executives, monitor assets, and upgrade yields.

Shrewd urban areas influence innovation to work on metropolitan living and arrive at a more extensive populace. IoT gadgets, sensors, and information examination add to proficient transportation frameworks, squander the executives, and energy utilization. Resident commitment stages empower occupants to partake in dynamic cycles, cultivating a feeling of local area and inclusivity.

The development of man-made brainpower (artificial intelligence) and AI (ML) has additionally enhanced the effect of innovation in contacting more extensive crowds. Artificial intelligence calculations investigate huge datasets to customize client encounters, anticipate inclinations, and suggest content. Chatbots and remote helpers offer moment and robotized help, upgrading client support and commitment for an enormous scope.

Notwithstanding, the far and wide reception of innovation additionally raises concerns connected with advanced consideration and access abberations. The computerized partition, described by inconsistent admittance to innovation and the web, can block endeavors to contact more extensive crowds. Overcoming this issue requires purposeful endeavors to guarantee that mechanical headways benefit all sections of society.

Security and protection contemplations likewise come to the cutting edge as innovation works with the assortment and trade of tremendous measures of individual information. Protecting client data, executing vigorous network safety gauges, and advancing computerized proficiency are fundamental parts of mindful and moral innovation use.

All in all, the use of innovation to contact more extensive crowds saturates each part of present day life, from training and business to amusement, medical services, and then some. The interconnectedness worked with by innovation has changed how data is shared, items are showcased, and administrations are conveyed, adding to a more interconnected and open worldwide scene. As innovation keeps on developing, there is a proceeded with need for moral contemplations, inclusivity, and computerized proficiency to guarantee that the advantages of innovation are acknowledged by different populaces all over the planet.

6.3 The dos and don'ts of integrating technology into speeches and presentations

Incorporating innovation into talks and introductions has turned into a typical work on, offering speakers and moderators a scope of instruments to improve commitment, pass on data really, and leave an enduring effect on their crowd. Notwithstanding, exploring the scene of innovation openly talking requires a smart methodology, taking into account both the benefits and possible traps. Grasping the customs of coordinating innovation into addresses and introductions is essential for making progress in correspondence.

The Dos

1. **Figure out Your Crowd:**

   Do: Designer your utilization of innovation to the inclinations and assumptions for your crowd. Consider factors like age, technical education, and the setting of the show. A well informed crowd could see the value in intelligent components, while a more conventional setting might require a more clear methodology.

2. **Utilize Drawing in Visuals:**

   Do: Consolidate excellent visuals to supplement your message. Use slides, pictures, and infographics to make complex data more available. Visuals can improve crowd understanding and maintenance, making your show more significant.

3. **Use Intelligent Devices:**

   Do: Connect with your crowd by consolidating intuitive components. Surveys, reviews, and back and forth discussions through computerized stages can make a more unique and participatory experience. Intelligent devices support crowd association and upgrade by and large commitment.

4. **Practice Mechanical Capability:**

   Do: Dive more deeply into the innovation you intend to utilize. Work on running your show on the picked stage, test sound and visual parts, and investigate likely issues. Being innovatively capable ingrains certainty and guarantees a smoother show.

5. **Guarantee Openness:**

   Do: Focus on openness in your mechanical decisions. Guarantee that any visuals or sight and sound components are clear and effectively perceptible by all crowd individuals. Consider openness highlights, like shut subtitling, to oblige assorted needs.

6. **Keep up with Availability Reinforcement:**

   Do: Get ready for likely specialized misfires by having a plan B. Convey a convenient charger for gadgets, have disconnected reinforcements of your show, and be prepared to change to elective techniques in the event that there are network issues. Being arranged shows amazing skill.

7. **Make a Consistent Incorporation:**

    Do: Incorporate innovation consistently into your show. Keep away from unexpected advances or mishandling with gadgets. Practice the progression of your show to guarantee that innovation improves your message without turning into an interruption.

8. **Empower Crowd Connection:**

    Do: Influence innovation to encourage crowd connection. Utilize live surveys, visit highlights, or virtual entertainment stages to support questions, remarks, and continuous commitment. Interfacing with your crowd improves the general insight.

9. **Recount a Convincing Story:**

    Do: Use innovation as a narrating device. Whether through visuals, recordings, or mixed media components, make a story that charms your crowd. A convincing story, supported by innovation, can have an enduring impression.

10. **Look for Criticism:**

Do: After your show, look for input on the mechanical angles. Comprehend what functioned admirably and recognize regions for development. Constant criticism permits you to refine your methodology and upgrade the adequacy of innovation in ongoing introductions.

The Don'ts

1. **Over-burden with Data:**

    Try not to: Oppose the compulsion to over-burden your show with inordinate data or complex visuals. Jumbled slides or overpowering interactive media components can occupy from your message and reduce crowd cognizance.

2. **Depend Entirely on Innovation:**

    Try not to: Rely altogether upon innovation to convey your message. Have a contingency plan for situations where innovation might come up short. Your capacity to pass on your message ought not be dependent upon the faultless presentation of gadgets or programming.

3. **Dismiss Specialized Checks:**

    Try not to: Forget to perform careful specialized actually looks at before your show. Guarantee that all gadgets, programming, and web associations are working consistently. Specialized errors can disturb the stream and effect the general adequacy of your show.

4. **Misjudge Crowd Variety:**

   Try not to: Expect a uniform degree of innovative capability among your crowd. Abstain from utilizing profoundly specialized language without giving setting. Guarantee that your innovative decisions are comprehensive and open to all crowd individuals.

5. **Overlook Using time effectively:**

   Try not to: Let innovation undermine your using time effectively. Work on pacing your show to take into consideration smooth changes between slides or media components. Being aware of time guarantees that your message is conveyed actually without surging or hauling.

6. **Use Innovation as an Interruption:**

   Try not to: Permit innovation to turn into an interruption. While visuals and mixed media components can upgrade commitment, an extreme spotlight on innovation might redirect consideration from your key message. Keep an equilibrium to keep the crowd zeroed in on the substance.

7. **Ignore Tasteful Contemplations:**

   Try not to: Neglect the tasteful parts of your show. Ineffectively planned slides, bungled variety plans, or indecipherable textual styles can reduce the visual allure and amazing skill of your show. An outwardly satisfying show adds to a positive crowd insight.

8. **Disregard Network Issues:**

   Try not to: Disregard the potential for network issues. Be ready to change to disconnected modes or elective strategies assuming there are difficulties with web network. Expecting and resolving these issues proactively limits interruptions during your show.

9. **Underplay Crowd Commitment:**

   Try not to: Underrate the significance of crowd commitment. While innovation can improve cooperation, it shouldn't supplant real association with your crowd. Keep in touch, answer crowd signs, and guarantee a harmony among innovation and individual commitment.

10. **Use Innovation for the good of its Own:**

Try not to: Coordinate innovation just for it. Each mechanical component ought to fill a need in improving your message. Stay away from superfluous devices or highlights that don't contribute genuinely to the general effect of your show.

6.4 Successful use of multimedia in communication

The fruitful utilization of sight and sound in correspondence has turned into a sign of compelling and connecting with informing across different spaces. Sight and sound, enveloping a scope of components like text, pictures, sound, video, and intelligent substance, has the ability to pass on data in a dynamic and convincing way. Whether in training, business, promoting, news coverage, or diversion, the essential reconciliation of sight and sound improves correspondence, enraptures crowds, and works with a more profound comprehension of the message.

In the domain of training, mixed media has reformed conventional showing strategies, establishing dynamic and intelligent learning conditions. Instructive organizations influence mixed media components, including instructive recordings, livelinesss, intuitive recreations, and computerized reading material, to improve the instructive experience. These devices take care of different learning styles, making complex ideas more open and encouraging a really captivating growing experience.

Visual guides, as outlines, diagrams, and infographics, supplement literary data, supporting the appreciation and maintenance of scholastic substance. E-learning stages and Monstrous Open Web-based Courses (MOOCs) use media broadly, furnishing students with the adaptability to get to instructive assets from any-place on the planet. The reconciliation of sight and sound in training democratizes advancing as well as gets ready understudies for a computerized driven future.

In the corporate scene, effective correspondence frequently relies on the essential utilization of sight and sound components. Business introductions, reports, and advertising materials benefit from the fuse of visuals, outlines, and charts to convey complex information and experiences. Mixed media components improve the clearness of correspondence, it isn't simply seen yet additionally made sure to guarantee that data.

Sight and sound introductions in business settings work with commitment and collaboration. Intelligent components, like interactive charts or implanted record-ings, can make introductions more powerful, cultivating a more participatory encounter. Besides, mixed media is an integral asset in preparing and improve-ment programs, permitting associations to make drawing in and powerful learning modules for representatives.

Showcasing, specifically, has gone through an extraordinary shift with the fruit-ful joining of sight and sound. The ascent of computerized showcasing stages, vir-tual entertainment, and web based publicizing has raised the significance of visuals in passing on brand messages. Recordings, infographics, and intelligent substance assume a urgent part in catching and holding the consideration of main interest groups in an undeniably serious computerized scene.

Narrating, improved by interactive media components, has turned into a focal part of effective showcasing efforts. Brands use recordings to describe convincing stories, summon feelings, and fabricate areas of strength for a character. Visual sub-stance via web-based entertainment stages, like Instagram and Pinterest, empowers brands to interface with their crowd on an individual level, encouraging brand dependability and commitment.

The gaming business is a perfect representation of the vivid and intuitive capa-bility of media. Computer games consistently coordinate illustrations, sound, and intuitive components to make virtual universes that enrapture players. Top notch illustrations, sensible movements, and convincing stories add to the outcome of computer games, making them a prevailing type of diversion.

Web-based features have reformed the manner in which media content, including films, Network programs, and music, is consumed. Stages like Netflix, Hulu, and Spotify influence interactive media to give on-request admittance to a tremendous library of content. The outcome of these stages is credited to their capacity to offer a customized and vivid survey insight, taking special care of individual inclinations.

News coverage and news revealing have advanced altogether with the mix of interactive media. Advanced news stages use recordings, intuitive illustrations, and live updates to upgrade the narrating part of news stories. Sight and sound components give a more thorough comprehension of information occasions, empowering crowds to draw in with content in a more vivid way.

Information perception, through infographics and intuitive outlines, has turned into a urgent part of current news coverage. Complex informational indexes are refined into outwardly engaging and open organizations, permitting perusers to rapidly get a handle on data. Media in reporting improves the introduction of information as well as adds to the democratization of data, contacting a more extensive crowd through web-based stages.

Imaginative articulation has been reclassified through the effective utilization of media in the domain of craftsmanship and inventiveness. Computerized workmanship, augmented reality establishments, and intelligent displays push the limits of customary fine arts. Specialists influence mixed media instruments to make vivid encounters that draw in various faculties, furnishing crowds with an extraordinary and participatory imaginative experience.

The web fills in as a worldwide material for craftsmen to grandstand their work, rising above geological limits. Online entertainment stages give an immediate channel to specialists to interface with their crowd, share their innovative flow, and earn respect. The democratization of creative articulation through computerized stages permits arising craftsmen to track down a worldwide crowd without the limitations of conventional watchmen.

Sight and sound innovations likewise assume a fundamental part in medical care correspondence. Clinical experts use visuals, like pictures and recordings, to clarify complex operations and conditions for patients. Patient training materials are upgraded with interactive media components, enabling people to comprehend their medical issue and therapy choices all the more extensively.

Telemedicine, fueled by mixed media specialized instruments, empowers far off counsels and virtual medical care administrations. Specialists can outwardly survey patients, share clinical pictures, and give constant direction through video conferencing. This not just further develops admittance to medical care, especially in remote or underserved regions yet in addition upgrades the general patient experience.

The combination of media in ecological correspondence has become progressively critical. Complex natural issues are imparted to people in general through perceptions, intuitive guides, and narratives. Media components add to a superior comprehension of the effect of human exercises on the climate, cultivating mindfulness and support for economical practices.

Innovation driven progressions, like computer generated experience (VR) and increased reality (AR), have additionally extended the potential outcomes of effective media correspondence. VR permits clients to drench themselves in virtual conditions, giving a profoundly intuitive and drawing in experience. AR overlays advanced data onto this present reality, offering new aspects to narrating and communication.

Computerized reasoning (artificial intelligence) is one more groundbreaking power in sight and sound correspondence. Man-made intelligence calculations break down client conduct, inclinations, and connections to customize interactive media content. Remote helpers, fueled by simulated intelligence, furnish clients with custom fitted proposals and reactions, improving the general client experience.

Regardless of the heap advantages of interactive media, certain difficulties and contemplations should be recognized. The potential for data over-burden is a worry, particularly when media components are not cautiously organized and may overpower the crowd. Furthermore, issues connected with the legitimacy and validity of sight and sound substance, especially in the time of deepfakes and controlled visuals, require watchful consideration.

Chapter 7

Evolving as a Master Communicator

Successful correspondence is an expertise that rises above time and stays a fundamental part of human collaboration. In the consistently advancing scene of correspondence, dominating this expertise becomes essential for outcome in different parts of life. Whether in private connections, proficient settings, or cultural elements, being an expert communicator can open entryways, cultivate understanding, and make ready for positive results.

Correspondence is certainly not a static idea; it develops with the changing elements of society, innovation, and culture. As we explore the 21st 100 years, the difficulties and amazing open doors introduced by correspondence have developed dramatically. To be an expert communicator in this complicated and dynamic climate requires flexibility, compassion, and a profound comprehension of the subtleties of human connection.

One vital part of developing as an expert communicator is embracing the headways in innovation that shape the manner in which we associate and convey our considerations. The computerized age has introduced another period of correspondence, portrayed by texting, online entertainment stages, and virtual connections. While these apparatuses have made correspondence more open, they likewise present difficulties concerning legitimacy and significant association.

In the domain of expert correspondence, the capacity to explore computerized stages and influence them really is a sign of an expert communicator. Whether it's making convincing messages, taking part in virtual gatherings, or using online entertainment for systems administration, the proficient communicator grasps the subtleties of every medium. They perceive that successful correspondence goes past the words utilized; it envelops tone, non-verbal communication (even in virtual settings), and the capacity to convey complex thoughts with clearness.

In addition, dominating advanced correspondence includes being aware of the likely traps, like distortion and the deficiency of non-verbal prompts. Emojis and emoticons, however generally utilized, may not necessarily convey the planned feelings precisely. An expert communicator, hence, improves the ability of communicating feelings and subtleties unequivocally, even without eye to eye connection.

In private connections, the advancement of correspondence is similarly significant. The approach of cell phones and web-based entertainment has adjusted the scene of how people interface and keep up with connections. The expert communicator perceives the requirement for balance — utilizing innovation to improve, not supplant, certified human association. They comprehend that the steady blast of notices and messages can prompt interruption and obstruct significant discussions.

To develop as an expert communicator in private connections, one must likewise be receptive to the feelings of others. Sympathy assumes a significant part in understanding and answering the sensations of those we speak with. The capacity to listen effectively, without judgment, encourages a feeling of trust and receptiveness. In a period where capacities to focus are contracting, the expertise of really hearing others turns into an uncommon and significant resource.

Besides, dominating correspondence in private connections includes exploring through clashes with artfulness. Conflicts are inescapable, however an expert communicator approaches them with a guarantee to grasping alternate points of view and figuring out some shared interest. They perceive that compelling compromise isn't tied in with winning a contention yet about safeguarding the relationship and encouraging shared development.

The work environment, with its different cluster of characters and jobs, presents an interesting arrangement of difficulties for correspondence. An expert communicator in an expert setting is skilled at fitting their message to various crowds, whether it's tending to colleagues, introducing to chiefs, or drawing in with clients. They comprehend that viable correspondence isn't one-size-fits-all; it requires a nuanced approach that thinks about the necessities and assumptions for different partners.

Authority correspondence, specifically, requests a dominance of both verbal and non-verbal signs. A pioneer who can move and propel through their words, signals, and presence significantly affects group elements. The capacity to convey a convincing vision, give clear guidelines, and deal productive criticism recognizes an expert communicator in an influential position.

In the domain of business, viable correspondence stretches out past the verbally expressed or composed word. Exchange, an expertise urgent for outcome in different fields, depends vigorously on the capacity to peruse and answer the prompts of others. An expert communicator in exchange figures out the force of quietness, the significance of non-verbal communication, and the essential utilization of language to accomplish wanted results.

Besides, as organizations work in a globalized world, culturally diverse correspondence turns into a basic part of progress. The expert communicator perceives and regards social subtleties, staying away from possible errors and building solid, commonly gainful connections. They are receptive to the way that motions, articulations, and, surprisingly, the understanding of time can change fundamentally across societies.

The advancing scene of correspondence additionally brings to the front the significance of legitimacy. In a world barraged with data and messages, people float towards the individuals who speak with genuineness and straightforwardness. The expert communicator grasps the worth of genuineness in building trust and believability, both actually and expertly.

Genuine correspondence includes adjusting one's words to their qualities and activities. It requires weakness, the ability to offer authentic viewpoints and feelings, regardless of whether they make us anxious. In a general public that frequently underlines flawlessness, the realness of an expert communicator stands apart as a guide of certified association.

The development of correspondence additionally focuses on the force of narrating. Whether in a meeting room, a homeroom, or an easygoing discussion, the capacity to recount a convincing story improves the effect of the message. The expert communicator winds around stories that reverberate with the crowd, making data noteworthy and moving activity.

In the period of data over-burden, where consideration is a scant asset, the specialty of narrating turns into an essential device for catching and keeping up with commitment. An expert communicator grasps the components of a decent story — an engaging hero, a convincing plot, and a significant goal. They perceive that accounts have the ability to summon feelings, invigorate interest, and have an enduring impression.

As correspondence keeps on advancing, so does the significance of computerized proficiency. The expert communicator isn't just capable in that frame of mind of correspondence yet additionally skilled at exploring the computerized scene.

This incorporates figuring out the calculations that shape online perceivability, perceiving the effect of web-based entertainment on open insight, and knowing among tenable and untrustworthy wellsprings of data.

Computerized education additionally envelops the capacity to fundamentally assess data and impart in a period of falsehood. The expert communicator is an insightful purchaser and maker of content, mindful of the obligation that accompanies molding stories in the computerized domain. They comprehend that deception can have sweeping results and effectively add to advancing precision and truth.

With regards to virtual entertainment, where people and associations have a worldwide stage, the expert communicator practices wariness and mindfulness. They perceive the lastingness of online substance and the possible reach of their words. Virtual entertainment, when utilized in a calculated way, can be an incredible asset for systems administration, promotion, and impact. An expert communicator use these stages to enhance their message and interface with a more extensive crowd.

The advancement of correspondence likewise highlights the significance of non-stop learning. An expert communicator perceives that remaining important in a quickly impacting world requires a guarantee to deep rooted learning. This incorporates remaining informed about arising innovations, cultural patterns, and correspondence methodologies. The capacity to adjust and gain from encounters positions the expert communicator as a dynamic and versatile power in the steadily moving scene of correspondence.

Advancing likewise includes looking for input and being available to useful analysis. The expert communicator comprehends that development comes from reflection and refinement. Whether it's through proper assessments, casual discussions, or self-appraisal, they effectively look for experiences into what their correspondence style means for other people and make deliberate changes.

Besides, the development of correspondence requires an uplifted familiarity with moral contemplations. The expert communicator works with trustworthiness, perceiving the effect of their words on people and networks. They are aware of the expected results of their correspondence and endeavor to maintain moral principles in all cooperations.

Moral correspondence includes regarding the protection and respect of others, staying away from control or duplicity, and advancing inclusivity and variety. In an interconnected world, where the results of correspondence can be significant, the expert communicator perceives the requirement for mindful and moral commitment.

The dominance of correspondence is additionally reflected in the capacity to oversee and use feelings. Genuinely canny correspondence includes figuring out one's own feelings, understanding the feelings of others, and utilizing this attention to really explore communications. The expert communicator stays created under tension, oversees struggle with respect, and encourages a positive profound environment in different settings.

7.1 Continual improvement and learning in the art of communication

Persistent improvement and learning in the specialty of correspondence is a deep rooted venture that unfurls in different features of our lives. In a world described by quick change, dynamic connections, and developing advancements, the capacity to convey really isn't simply an expertise; it is a competitive edge. This excursion of progress includes a guarantee to continuous learning, an eagerness to embrace new viewpoints, and an acknowledgment that the specialty of correspondence is rarely static.

One primary component of constant improvement in correspondence is the development of mindfulness. Understanding one's correspondence style, assets, and regions for improvement is significant. This mindfulness reaches out to perceiving what our words and activities mean for other people. It includes pondering the criticism we get and effectively looking for open doors for self-reflection.

Mindful communicators are aware of their non-verbal signs, manner of speaking, and the effect of their presence in different settings. This mindfulness permits them to change their correspondence style in view of the specific situation and the necessities of those they are communicating with. It is a foundation of viable correspondence, empowering people to construct compatibility, explore social elements, and pass on messages with clearness and effect.

One more key part of consistent improvement in correspondence is the acknowledgment that it is a two-way road. Undivided attention is an expertise that supports significant communications. The expert communicator conveys their contemplations actually as well as listens mindfully to other people. This includes suspending judgment, keeping a receptive outlook, and trying to grasp alternate points of view.

Undivided attention goes past hearing words; it includes deciphering tone, figuring out feelings, and getting a handle on the fundamental messages. The ceaseless student in correspondence improves their listening abilities through training and a certified interest in others. They perceive that powerful correspondence isn't just about communicating one's thoughts yet in addition about making a space for others to be heard and perceived.

As innovation keeps on reshaping the correspondence scene, keeping up to date with computerized progressions is critical for nonstop improvement. The cutting edge communicator comprehends the subtleties of virtual correspondence, whether it's through video conferencing,

messages, or cooperative internet based stages. They perceive the difficulties of conveying feelings and building associations in a computerized climate and effectively look for ways of upgrading their virtual relational abilities.

Computerized proficiency is a part of constant improvement, including the capacity to explore online entertainment, observe tenable data from falsehood, and influence innovation for successful correspondence. The authority of computerized correspondence includes involving the most recent apparatuses as well as figuring out the effect of advanced cooperations on connections and discernments.

In the expert circle, persistent improvement in correspondence is intently attached to authority adequacy. Pioneers who focus on correspondence as a center capability cultivate a positive hierarchical culture, rouse their groups, and explore difficulties with artfulness. Initiative correspondence includes lucidity of vision, the capacity to spur others, and a pledge to straightforwardness.

Pioneers who ceaselessly look to further develop their relational abilities effectively request criticism from their groups, partake in proficient improvement potential open doors, and adjust their correspondence methodologies to the advancing requirements of the association. They perceive that compelling initiative correspondence is certainly not a one-size-fits-all undertaking; it requires adaptability and a consciousness of the different points of view inside the group.

Constant improvement additionally includes the essential utilization of criticism. Productive analysis, whether got officially through execution assessments or casually through relational collaborations, gives important experiences to development. The expert communicator embraces input as a chance for picking up, perceiving that even helpful analysis is a pathway to progress.

In addition, the consistent student in correspondence effectively searches out tutors and good examples. Gaining from the individuals who have become amazing at correspondence gives important bits of knowledge and direction. Mentorship connections offer a stage for getting customized criticism, acquiring pragmatic exhortation, and exploring the intricacies of different correspondence situations.

Ceaseless improvement in correspondence reaches out to the composed word. Whether making messages, reports, or other composed records, successful composing is an expertise that requires continuous refinement. The expert communicator focuses on lucidity, succinctness, and the general effect of their composed correspondence. They perceive that composed messages, as expressed words, pass on data as well as the tone and incredible skill of the communicator.

Moreover, the consistent student in correspondence comprehends the force of narrating in composed and oral correspondence. The capacity to pass data on through story connects with the crowd, makes the message noteworthy, and adds a human touch to correspondence. Whether in business introductions, instructive settings, or easygoing discussions, the craft of narrating is an amazing asset for catching consideration and cultivating understanding.

In the domain of relational connections, nonstop improvement includes exploring the intricacies of feelings and compromise. Genuinely keen correspondence is an expertise that remains closely connected with mindfulness. The expert communicator perceives and deals with their feelings while likewise being sensitive to the sensations of others. The capacity to understand people on a profound level adds to building trust, settling clashes, and establishing a positive close to home environment in different settings.

Struggle is an unavoidable part of human collaboration, and the nonstop student in correspondence approaches it with a productive outlook. Compromise includes undivided attention, sympathy, and a pledge to tracking down commonly useful arrangements. It requires the capacity to isolate the individual from the issue, center around shared objectives, and speak with deference and consideration.

Persistent improvement in correspondence additionally includes social ability. In an interconnected existence where various societies converge, the expert communicator perceives and regards social subtleties. They comprehend that correspondence styles, motions, and, surprisingly, the translation of time can change essentially across societies. Social capability includes adjusting correspondence techniques to establish a comprehensive and deferential climate.

Furthermore, the nonstop student in correspondence is proficient at dealing with their web-based presence. In the period of virtual entertainment, people and associations have a computerized impression that adds to their public picture. The expert communicator explores virtual entertainment stages with purposefulness, perceiving the possible effect of their internet based associations on private and expert connections.

Fabricating and keeping a positive internet based standing includes insightful substance curation, commitment with a different crowd, and a consciousness of the likely outcomes of online correspondence. The dominance of computerized decorum and the capacity to use online entertainment for systems administration and expert development are vital parts of persistent improvement in correspondence.

In instructive settings, the craft of correspondence stretches out to educating and learning. Instructors who ceaselessly look to further develop their relational abilities establish a positive learning climate for their understudies. Compelling educating includes clearness of guidance, dynamic commitment, and the capacity to convey complex ideas with straightforwardness.

Ceaseless improvement in correspondence for instructors incorporates keeping up to date with imaginative showing techniques, coordinating innovation into the opportunity for growth, and adjusting to the different learning styles of understudies. The expert communicator in schooling cultivates a homeroom climate where understudies feel appreciated, esteemed, and motivated to participate in the educational experience.

Besides, the specialty of correspondence crosses with support and public talking. Whether supporting for a purpose, conveying a feature address, or partaking in open discussions, the persistent student in correspondence improves their public talking abilities. This includes becoming the best at influence, spellbinding a crowd of people, and passing on messages with conviction and realness.

Public talking isn't just about verbal correspondence; it incorporates non-verbal communication, tone, and the capacity to associate sincerely with the crowd. The expert communicator perceives the effect of their presence in front of an audience and effectively looks for chances to refine their public abilities to talk. They comprehend that compelling public talking has the ability to motivate activity, impact feelings, and have an enduring impression.

7.2 Seeking and incorporating feedback for personal growth

Looking for and integrating input for self-improvement is a dynamic and fundamental part of personal growth that rises above different features of life. Whether in proficient undertakings, instructive pursuits, or individual connections, the capacity to request, get, and apply criticism is a strong impetus for individual turn of events. This cycle includes a blend of self-reflection, modesty, and a veritable obligation to constant learning.

At its center, looking for input is a functioning and deliberate work to acquire bits of knowledge into one's assets, regions for development, and the effect of one's activities on others. It requires an eagerness to step outside one's usual range of familiarity and welcome helpful analysis, recognizing that development frequently emerges from the acknowledgment of regions where improvement is conceivable.

The most common way of looking for input starts with a groundwork of mindfulness. Figuring out one's own assets, shortcomings, and personal conduct standards gives a beginning stage to looking for designated and significant criticism. Mindful people are better prepared to form explicit inquiries and areas of center while requesting criticism, bringing about additional noteworthy experiences.

In proficient settings, the quest for criticism is firmly entwined with profession advancement. Representatives who effectively look for criticism exhibit a pledge to individual and expert development. This proactive methodology not just encourages a culture of constant improvement inside associations yet in addition positions people for progression and outcome in their vocations.

In the work environment, the most common way of looking for criticism frequently includes drawing in with managers, associates, and subordinates. The capacity to explore progressive designs and look for input according to different viewpoints is an expertise in itself. The seasoned veteran at looking for criticism perceives the worth of assorted perspectives and effectively looks for input from people at various levels inside the association.

Moreover, the readiness to look for input is characteristic of a development mentality — a conviction that capacities and knowledge can be created through devotion and difficult work. People with a development outlook view moves as any open doors to learn and embrace input for the purpose of refining their abilities. This mentality cultivates strength and flexibility despite misfortunes.

The most common way of looking for criticism is a complementary one. People who effectively look for criticism from others are much of the time apparent as agreeable and open to coordinated effort. This transparency makes a good criticism circle where partners feel open to giving info, adding to a culture of nonstop improvement inside the association.

In instructive settings, the quest for criticism is vital to the growing experience. Understudies who effectively look for input on their scholarly execution, tasks, and activities gain significant bits of knowledge into their assets and regions for development. This proactive methodology adds to a more profound comprehension of the topic and upgrades by and large learning results.

Besides, the capacity to look for input from educators and companions cultivates a cooperative and steady learning climate. It advances a culture where clarifying some pressing issues and looking for explanation are seen as proactive strides toward progress as opposed to indications of shortcoming. The consistent student in instructive settings perceives that criticism is an important asset for scholastic development.

In private connections, looking for criticism assumes a vital part in relational elements. Successful correspondence inside connections includes figuring out the effect of one's words and activities on others. People who effectively look for input from their companions, family, and accomplices exhibit a promise to understanding and answering the requirements and points of view of those they care about.

In close connections, the capacity to request and consolidate criticism adds to shared understanding and development. It includes being responsive to helpful analysis, conveying transparently about assumptions, and effectively pursuing gathering each other's necessities. The constant student in private connections perceives that criticism is a device for reinforcing associations and settling clashes.

The most common way of looking for criticism isn't without its difficulties. It requires a degree of weakness and modesty to welcome info that might feature regions for development. Beating the feeling of dread toward analysis and reevaluating criticism as a chance for development is fundamental. People who embrace criticism as a useful instrument for improvement are better situated to explore the intricacies of individual and expert connections.

Moreover, the most common way of looking for criticism is best when combined with a certifiable longing to consolidate the bits of knowledge acquired. It includes a functioning and purposeful work to apply the criticism got, make acclimations to conduct or practices, and track progress after some time. The eagerness to follow up on criticism is a vital differentiator between the people who latently get information and the individuals who effectively influence it for self-improvement.

In the expert domain, the fuse of criticism frequently includes the advancement of an activity plan. People who get input from execution assessments, project surveys, or companion evaluations can utilize this data to lay out unambiguous objectives for development. The capacity to make a guide for development exhibits a proactive way to deal with individual and expert turn of events.

Furthermore, consolidating input might include looking for extra assets, preparing, or mentorship to address recognized regions for development. The ceaseless student in proficient settings perceives that self-improvement is a continuous excursion that requires a mix of independent endeavors and outside help. This might incorporate going to studios, chasing after additional instruction, or looking for direction from tutors who can give important bits of knowledge.

In instructive settings, the consolidation of criticism is intently attached to the iterative idea of the educational experience. Understudies who get criticism on tasks or tests have the chance to refine how they might interpret the material and improve their scholarly presentation. The use of input includes an intelligent cycle where understudies evaluate their work, recognize regions for development, and effectively pursue dominance.

In addition, the fuse of criticism in training reaches out past grades and appraisals. It includes creating metacognitive abilities — the capacity to consider and manage one's own reasoning. Understudies who effectively look for and consolidate criticism become more capable at perceiving designs in their picking up, figuring out their mental cycles, and making key changes in accordance with improve their scholastic achievement.

In private connections, the consolidation of criticism is a cooperative exertion. It includes open correspondence, an eagerness to address concerns raised by others, and a guarantee to self-awareness to help the relationship. Couples or relatives who effectively cooperate to apply criticism add to the improvement of a solid and strong security.

The ceaseless student in private connections perceives that development is a common excursion. It includes tending to individual regions for development as well as cultivating a climate where common criticism adds to the general prosperity of the relationship. This cooperative methodology assembles trust, upgrades correspondence, and fortifies the underpinning of special interactions.

Input, when successfully looked for and integrated, turns into an impetus for self-awareness. It fills in as a mirror that mirrors one's assets and regions for development, giving a guide to improvement. The ceaseless student comprehends that the most common way of looking for and consolidating criticism is certainly not a one-time occasion yet a repeating and progressing venture towards greatness.

Besides, the combination of criticism is a demonstration of flexibility and versatility. It requires the capacity to embrace change, gain from encounters, and make deliberate acclimations to conduct and practices. The seasoned veteran at looking for and consolidating criticism sees misfortunes as any open doors for picking up, perceiving that conquering difficulties adds to individual and expert development.

7.3 Staying adaptable to evolving communication trends

Remaining versatile to developing correspondence patterns is a urgent expertise in the consistently changing scene of human collaboration. In this present reality where innovation, culture, and cultural elements ceaselessly reshape how we associate, impart, and share data, the capacity to adjust is fundamental for viable and significant commitment. Whether in private connections, proficient settings, or the more extensive advanced circle, remaining versatile guarantees that people stay important and receptive to the developing necessities of correspondence.

The quick development of innovation has essentially influenced correspondence patterns. From the appearance of the web to the expansion of cell phones and the ascent of online entertainment, every development has reshaped the manner in which individuals impart. Adjusting to these mechanical movements includes gaining new abilities as well as grasping the ramifications of these progressions on correspondence elements.

In proficient settings, remaining versatile to advancing correspondence patterns implies exploring the computerized scene with capability. The dominance of email correspondence, video conferencing stages, and cooperative instruments is currently pretty much as fundamental as customary verbal and composed relational abilities. The versatile communicator perceives that successful connection requires a mix of both conventional and computerized specialized strategies.

Additionally, as virtual correspondence turns out to be progressively common, remaining versatile includes grasping the subtleties of remote work and virtual cooperation. The capacity to convey thoughts obviously written down, explore virtual gatherings with incredible skill, and influence innovation for consistent correspondence are abilities that put versatile communicators aside in the advanced proficient scene.

In private connections, the effect of developing correspondence patterns is apparent in how individuals associate and keep up with associations. The ascent of web-based entertainment stages, texting applications, and online networks has extended the manners in which people communicate. Adjusting to these patterns includes understanding the job of these stages in encouraging associations while being aware of possible entanglements, like the gamble of miscommunication and the effect of advanced connections on connections.

The versatile communicator in private connections perceives the requirement for balance. While innovation gives advantageous ways of remaining associated, enhancing virtual cooperations with eye to eye communication is fundamental. Adjusting to developing correspondence patterns includes involving innovation as an instrument to improve, not supplant, certified human association.

Besides, remaining versatile to advancing correspondence patterns requires a comprehension of the effect of visual and sight and sound components. The ascent of visual correspondence through pictures, recordings, and emoticons has become essential to passing on feelings and upgrading messages. Versatile communicators perceive the force of visual narrating and integrate it into their correspondence procedures to make their messages really captivating and significant.

In the computerized circle, remaining versatile includes a sharp familiarity with web-based entertainment patterns, calculations, and developing stages. The versatile communicator comprehends the significance of keeping a pertinent and legitimate internet based presence. This incorporates sharing substance as well as effectively taking part in web-based discussions, fabricating an individual brand, and utilizing virtual entertainment for systems administration and expert development.

The advancement of correspondence drifts additionally focuses on the significance of computerized education. Remaining versatile requires the capacity to basically assess data, perceive believable sources, and explore the intricacies of online talk. The versatile communicator isn't just capable in utilizing computerized apparatuses yet in addition cautious about the mindful and moral utilization of innovation in correspondence.

Besides, remaining versatile to developing correspondence patterns includes a ceaseless learning outlook. People who effectively look to grasp arising innovations, new correspondence stages, and changing social elements position themselves to be on the ball.

This obligation to learning guarantees that communicators stay spry and receptive to the developing requirements and inclinations of their crowd.

In proficient settings, the versatile communicator perceives the effect of globalization on correspondence. Diverse correspondence has turned into an indispensable expertise as organizations and associations work on a worldwide scale. Adjusting to different social standards, correspondence styles, and decorum is fundamental for viable coordinated effort and building solid, commonly useful connections.

The advancement of correspondence drifts additionally stresses the significance of realness. In a world immersed with data, people are attracted to communicators who convey genuineness and earnestness. Versatile communicators perceive the benefit of being certifiable in their cooperations, building trust through straightforward correspondence, and adjusting their words to their activities.

Credible correspondence includes an eagerness to show weakness, express certifiable feelings, and offer individual stories. Versatile communicators comprehend that legitimacy cultivates certifiable associations and resounds with crowds in our current reality where validness is progressively esteemed.

In instructive settings, remaining versatile to advancing correspondence patterns is fundamental for compelling educating and learning. The ascent of online training, advanced assets, and intuitive stages has changed the instructive scene. Versatile instructors influence these devices to make drawing in growth opportunities, work with coordinated effort, and take care of assorted learning styles.

Moreover, remaining versatile in training includes perceiving the changing assumptions for understudies. The advanced student is acquainted with getting to data quickly and favors intelligent and sight and sound rich substance. Versatile instructors integrate these inclinations into their showing procedures, embracing advanced apparatuses, and establishing dynamic learning conditions that take special care of the developing requirements of understudies.

Remaining versatile to developing correspondence drifts additionally includes perceiving the effect of data over-burden. In this present reality where people are barraged with immense measures of data, the versatile communicator figures out the significance of curtness, lucidity, and pertinence in their messages. Whether in composed or verbal correspondence, the capacity to pass on data succinctly while keeping up with influence is a sign of versatility.

Furthermore, remaining versatile in correspondence requires a comprehension of the advancing idea of emergency correspondence. In the midst of vulnerability or emergencies, the versatile communicator explores through difficulties with straightforwardness, compassion, and an essential methodology.

They perceive the significance of opportune and exact correspondence, the job of virtual entertainment in emergency correspondence, and the requirement for flexibility in answering quickly evolving conditions.

The persistent development of correspondence drifts likewise accentuates the significance of the ability to appreciate individuals on a deeper level. Versatile communicators grasp the job of feelings in human collaborations and effectively develop the ability to understand anyone on a profound level to really explore relational elements. This includes perceiving and managing one's own feelings, grasping the feelings of others, and utilizing this attention to direct correspondence methodologies.

In influential positions, remaining versatile to developing correspondence patterns is a vital part of compelling administration. Pioneers who can speak with nimbleness and credibility move trust, cultivate coordinated effort, and explore complex difficulties with strength. The versatile pioneer perceives the need to fit their correspondence style to various crowds, whether tending to colleagues, clients, or the more extensive public.

Initiative correspondence in the cutting edge period includes using an assortment of correspondence channels, from customary eye to eye gatherings to virtual municipal centers and online entertainment stages. Versatile pioneers influence these channels decisively to convey their vision, draw in with partners, and answer the developing assumptions for their crowd.

In addition, remaining versatile in administration correspondence includes perceiving the force of narrating. The capacity to convey a convincing story improves the effect of a pioneer's message, making it vital and motivating activity. Versatile pioneers comprehend the specialty of narrating and use it to interface with their crowd on a more profound level.

The nonstop student in correspondence likewise perceives the significance of criticism in authority improvement. Looking for and consolidating criticism from colleagues, companions, and tutors gives significant bits of knowledge that add to individual and expert development. Versatile pioneers view input as a helpful instrument for development and effectively develop a culture of open correspondence inside their groups.

7.4 Inspiring others through your words: the responsibility of a captivating communicator

Motivating others through your words is a significant obligation that rises above correspondence as a simple expertise and raises it to a work of art. An enamoring communicator comprehends the power implanted in language, perceiving that words can possibly summon feelings, shape viewpoints, and touch off extraordinary activities. Whether in private connections, influential positions, or public talking commitment, the capacity to move through words conveys a significant obligation — one that requires realness, compassion, and a profound comprehension of the effect words can have on people and networks.

In private connections, the obligation of rousing others through words is fundamental to encouraging association and building trust. The specialty of correspondence in private connections goes past passing on data; it includes communicating feelings, approving sentiments, and establishing a climate where people feel seen and heard. An enthralling communicator in private connections is receptive to the requirements and goals of others, utilizing words to elevate, empower, and impart certainty.

Additionally, moving others through words in private connections includes the capacity to explore troublesome discussions with elegance and compassion. The obligation of an enthralling communicator isn't just to pass positive messages yet in addition on to address difficulties, clashes, and delicate points with a pledge to understanding and goal. Words, when picked insightfully, can mend wounds, span holes, and fortify the bonds that structure the underpinning of significant associations.

In positions of authority, the obligation of moving others through words takes on a key and significant aspect. Pioneers who comprehend the heaviness of their words perceive that they are not only passing on data but rather forming the way of life and heading of their groups or associations. The capacity to explain a convincing vision, convey a feeling of direction, and spur others toward shared objectives recognizes a spellbinding communicator in an administrative role.

A pioneer's words can be a wellspring of motivation and inspiration, driving people to blow away their apparent restrictions. Whether tending to a group, conveying a feature discourse, or making composed correspondences, the obligation lies in rousing certainty, cultivating a positive hierarchical culture, and making a common feeling of direction that rises above individual commitments.

Notwithstanding vision projecting, an enthralling communicator in a position of authority likewise embraces straightforwardness and legitimacy. The obligation of moving others through words incorporates being open about difficulties, recognizing errors, and sharing individual accounts of versatility and development. This weakness cultivates trust and energizes a culture where colleagues feel open to embracing their own realness and adding to the aggregate achievement.

Public talking enhances the obligation of rousing others through words on a more extensive scale. Whether tending to a little gathering or an enormous crowd, an enthralling communicator perceives the possibility to influence hearts and brains. Public talking isn't just about conveying data; about making an encounter reverberates with the crowd, mixes feelings, and prompts reflection.

The obligation of a charming communicator openly talking includes cautious thought of the message, the crowd, and the ideal effect. Creating a convincing story, utilizing expository gadgets, and consolidating engaging tales are instruments that assist with enrapturing a group of people and have an enduring effect. The capacity to associate with different crowds and rouse them toward activity is a sign of an enthralling communicator out in the open talking commitment.

Moreover, the obligation of motivating others through words stretches out to the computerized domain, where online stages give a worldwide stage. Web-based entertainment, sites, and computerized content proposition a chance to contact a wide crowd and impact public talk. A dazzling communicator in the computerized space comprehends the expected reach of their words and embraces the obligation to contribute decidedly to online discussions.

In the computerized age, where data is spread quickly, the obligation of moving others through words incorporates truth checking, staying away from deception, and advancing a culture of advanced proficiency. A dazzling communicator use on-line stages to share significant bits of knowledge, encourage discourse, and add to a positive and informed internet based local area.

Morals assume an essential part in the obligation of moving others through words. A dazzling communicator works with uprightness, perceiving that the effect of their words stretches out past the quick setting. Moral correspondence includes genuineness, straightforwardness, and a guarantee to truth. It additionally incorporates regarding the security and nobility of people and staying away from the utilization of language that could propagate mischief or segregation.

The obligation of rousing others through words in the advanced domain additionally includes effectively captivating with the crowd. Answering remarks, cultivating a feeling of local area, and recognizing different points of view add to building a good web-based presence. The capacity to move and impact others through computerized correspondence requires viable message creating as well as a certifiable association with the crowd.

In instructive settings, the obligation of rousing others through words lies at the core of powerful educating and mentorship. Teachers who comprehend the effect of their words on understudies perceive that they are not simply spreading data but rather molding the scholarly and close to home advancement of people in the future. A spellbinding communicator in schooling utilizes words to light interest, invigorate decisive reasoning, and impart an adoration for learning.

Motivating others through words in training includes establishing a comprehensive and strong learning climate. The obligation stretches out to perceiving and esteeming different points of view, cultivating a culture of open exchange, and empowering understudies to offer their viewpoints and suppositions. A spellbinding communicator in schooling imparts a feeling of miracle, interest, and a deep rooted enthusiasm for information.

Moreover, the obligation of moving others through words in training incorporates adjusting helping methodologies to take care of assorted learning styles. Enrapturing teachers influence narrating, intelligent conversations, and interactive media assets to make connecting with growth opportunities. The capacity to pass complex ideas with lucidity and energy contributes on to making the instructive excursion rousing and essential for understudies.

The obligation of motivating others through words likewise includes mentorship. Coaches who comprehend the heaviness of their words perceive that they assume a crucial part in directing and molding the desires of their mentees. A spellbinding communicator in mentorship utilizes words to offer direction, share shrewdness, and impart trust in the capacities and capability of those they coach.

Notwithstanding the expressed or composed word, the obligation of moving others through words incorporates non-verbal correspondence. Non-verbal communication, looks, and motions supplement the expressed word, adding to the general effect of the message. An enamoring communicator focuses on these non-verbal signs, perceiving their job in conveying truthfulness, sympathy, and realness.

Sympathy is a fundamental component in the obligation of rousing others through words. A dazzling communicator comprehends the points of view and feelings of their crowd, fitting their message to resound with the encounters and yearnings of those they are tending to. Compassionate correspondence includes undivided attention, recognizing the sensations of others, and communicating getting it and backing.

Also, the obligation of motivating others through words incorporates perceiving the force of encouraging feedback. Recognizing accomplishments, offering thanks, and offering inspirational statements add to encouraging a positive and spurred climate. A spellbinding communicator figures out the effect of positive words on resolve, certainty, and the general prosperity of people and groups.